Davenport's Kentucky Wills And Estate Planning Legal Forms

DAVENPORT'S KENTUCKY WILLS AND ESTATE PLANNING LEGAL FORMS

2024 EDITION

written by attorneys
Alex Russell and Robert Maxwell

SEE BOOKS AND LEGAL FORMS AT WWW.DAVENPORTPUBLISHING.COM

COPYRIGHT © 2024 -- ALEX RUSSELL

CREATIVE COMMONS LICENSE. This work is also licensed under a Creative Commons Attribution-NonCommercial-NoDerivatives 4.0 International License.

GOVERNMENT WORKS. No claim is made to copyright or ownership of government materials.

SOME STANDARD FORMS. No copyright or ownership is claimed of "standard" forms or leading forms for the state which are provided in this book, but fair use and privilege to use is claimed. Makers of such forms (often a state agency or hospital) have agreed by word, act, and implication the forms may be used and copied if no profit is sought and no substantial changes made to them. Such makers if not a lawyer or law firm are barred from profit or advantage in practicing law by making forms then limiting use. Forms and other related materials are used here for educational purposes only. Authors strongly believe in a religious duty to help people and do charity.

PUBLICATION DATA
(informal, library may use different data)

Names: Russell, Alex, 1972- author; Maxwell, Robert, 1960- author

Title: Davenport's Kentucky Wills And Estate Planning Legal Forms 2024 Edition

Other Titles: Davenport's Wills

Description: Davenport Publishing 2024

Suggested Identifiers: 9798372471498, LCCN 2021909030, 9798748423373

Subjects: LCSH: Wills--United States;
Wills--United States--Forms;
Estate Planning--United States;
Legal Forms

Classification: LFF KF755 .C55 2024 (or as library chooses)
DDC 346.73 Rus--dc24 (or as library chooses)

9 8 7 6 5 4 3 2 1 0 0 0 0 0 2 4

PERMISSION TO COPY AND USE BOOKS FOR FREE

To help people and groups the publisher and authors of the book allow mostly free use by giving all a "Creative Commons Attribution-NonCommercial-NoDerivatives 4.0 International License". Most users face no limit on copying, using, holding in library to loan out, or giving out copies.

Basically, as the image below shows, any copying or use is OK if it still shows it is <u>by</u> the authors, is non-commercial (<u>nc</u>) with no price charged, and has no derivatives (<u>nd</u>) so no big changes.

(This work licensed under a Creative Commons Attribution-NonCommercial-NoDerivatives 4.0 International License.)

TO GET COPIES OF BOOKS USE WWW.DAVENPORTPUBLISHING.COM OR AMAZON.COM.

EMAIL ANY QUESTIONS TO DAVENPORTPRESS@GMAIL.COM.

WARNING

THIS PUBLICATION IS NOT A SUBSTITUTE FOR LEGAL ADVICE. Publisher and authors say and warn this publication is not giving any legal, accounting, or other professional services or advice, which if wanted can be obtained by consulting in person an attorney or some other professional. **<u>No attorney-client relationship or any relationship creating a duty or obligation is agreed to or created by the purchase or use of this publication or forms</u>.**

BOOKS AND FORMS FOR OTHER STATES ARE AVAILABLE.
SEE WWW.DAVENPORTPUBLISHING.COM FOR INFORMATION.

CHAPTER	TABLE OF CONTENTS	PAGE NUMBER
CH. 1 – LIST OF FORMS, BOOK BASICS, AND INFORMATION FORM		1
CH. 2 – LEGAL TERMS AND BASIC PROPERTY LAW		6
CH. 3 – WILL BASICS		8
CH. 4 – WILL GIFTS INCLUDING RESIDUE CLAUSE		10
CH. 5 – DEBT, FAMILY, SPOUSE, HOMESTEAD, AND CHILD ISSUES		15
CH. 6 – BASIC IDEAS ABOUT HEALTH CARE FORMS		18

WILL RELATED FORMS

CH. 7 – FORM 1: WILL (STANDARD)		19
CH. 8 – FORM 2: WILL (GUARDIAN)		23
CH. 9 – FORM 3: SELF-PROVING AFFIDAVIT		27
CH. 10 – FORM 4: HANDWRITTEN WILL		29

HEALTH CARE FORMS

CH. 11 – FORM 5: LIVING WILL DIRECTIVE AND HEALTH CARE SURROGATE DESIGNATION		31
CH. 12 – FORM 6: DO NOT RESUSCITATE		35

GIVING POWER FORMS

CH. 13 – FORM 7: STATUTORY FORM POWER OF ATTORNEY		41
CH. 14 – FORM 8: STANDARD POWER OF ATTORNEY FOR MEDICAL / SCHOOL DECISION MAKING		48
CH. 15 – FORM 9: FUNERAL PLANNING DECLARATION		50

APPENDIX – SAMPLE FILLED OUT LEGAL FORMS		54

CHAPTER 1
LIST OF FORMS, BOOK BASICS, AND INFORMATION FORM

ESTATE PLANNING CONTROLS THINGS IF LATER ABSENT, SICK, OR DEAD
From Davenport Publishing this book covers "Estate Planning", which is a person doing legal documents to control their health care, property, money, children, and funeral if the person is later absent, sick, or dead.

ESTATE PLANNING MOSTLY IS DOING SIMPLE THINGS IN 3 AREAS
Estate Planning is mostly doing simple things in 3 areas: Will Related, Health Care, and Giving Power. This book has many legal forms specially made for Kentucky. Most people use just a few of the forms.

WILL RELATED FORMS

Form 1. Will (Standard) – a Will (also called a "Last Will And Testament") lets a person control things after their death like who gets money and property, who is Executor, and if easier legal options are OK later.

Form 2. Will (Guardian) – this is a Will with part added to name a person to be Guardian to care for a minor child under 18 if needed (like if both parents later die) and also manage a child's property and money.

Form 3. Self-Proving Affidavit – optional form done with a Will to later help use the Will.

Form 4. Handwritten Will – this Will skips the usual 2 witnesses which saves some work, but all of it must be handwritten by the person doing the Will.

HEALTH CARE FORMS

Form 5. Living Will Directive And Health Care Surrogate Designation – lets a person 1) write care instructions and name someone as "Surrogate" to control health care if later needed (like if the person is later incapacitated by inability to be conscious or talk), and 2) say to stop most health care if a person is later incapacitated and later doctors think more care won't help (this is called a "Living Will" since it helps the living).

Form 6. Do Not Resuscitate – these are actually 2 forms that do the serious act of immediately refusing most care, and these are short so paramedics can read them fast and they can be used outside any facility.

GIVING POWER FORMS

Form 7. Statutory Form Power Of Attorney – lets power over money, property, and other things be shared during a person's life with a trusted person like a spouse, relative, or friend so they can do things.

Form 8. Standard Power Of Attorney For Medical/School Decision Making – lets parent give power over a child under age 18 with someone so they can make decisions about health care and school if needed.

Form 9. Funeral Planning Declaration – lets instructions be given and person be named to control funeral and related issues (if this form isn't done then by law a spouse or next closest relative does this).

KENTUCKY LAW ON ESTATE PLANNING COVERS MOST PEOPLE HERE

This book is only for Kentucky since Estate Planning laws and legal documents do vary among states. Kentucky law applies to Estate Planning usually if a person: a) has their main residence here (called their "domicile"), or b) resided here and left but always keeps firm plans to leave any new place (even if a person rents a home elsewhere like some students, military, and workers). Note, many people also do health care forms for the state a health facility they use is in. Most immigrants of any kind can do Estate Planning here.

PERSON HAS POWER TO CONTROL THESE THINGS BUT IT'S OFTEN NOT VITAL

Estate Planning to control health care, property, money, children, funeral, and similar things if a person is absent, sick, or dead is usually easy to do because a person mostly has full power to control these things. Given this usually judges, doctors, and other people mostly just ask: "Based on what a person wrote what did they likely want done?" It is also easy to do because simple legal documents can do the things and simple words can also be used (like listing some property and putting a few names). And despite what many people say often Estate Planning is not worth a lot of effort or money since it often doesn't greatly change the costs, taxes, delays, and later work that is needed. Benefits seem especially low for young people since only 4% of people die by age 50, and only 0.2% of children before age 18 have 2 parents die to need big legal help. Many people spend more energy and money on getting good life insurance to try to help family and friends.

BOOK IS SHORT, QUICKLY SHOWS LEGAL FORMS, AND USES EMPHASIS

This short book may read rough but it can be read fast and it also quickly shows people many legal forms. For emphasis some paragraph titles, boxes, and underlining is used, some small words are skipped, and end quote marks is put before punctuation. Though optional some legal words like Will and Testator are capitalized.

THIS BOOK COVERS THE MAIN LEGAL IDEAS AND SHOULD SUIT MOST PEOPLE

This book covers the main U.S. legal ideas on Estate Planning and most big ways Kentucky law is different. This book can't cover all legal issues but should suit most people without some strange situations or wishes. Strange situations or wishes that may need research or a lawyer include: a) strange gift wishes for property and money, b) wealth over $5 million, c) big medical concerns like extreme age, d) property or money going to a person with a disability or special needs, and e) wish to move or hide assets to qualify for government help.

FORMS MAKE BINDING LEGAL DOCUMENTS AND BOOK HAS STANDARD FORMS

Legal forms are good at most things involved in Estate Planning and can make binding legal documents. Instead of legal forms a lawyer can be used for Estate Planning but this can be costly, take months of work, and they can make mistakes. In life people often pick a cheaper option. Importantly, often a hospital, charity, state agency, or state legislature has made a form most people use and call the "standard form", and doctors, judges, and other people may not like to follow anything else. This book does provide mostly standard forms.

DOCUMENTS MAY NEED TO BE WITNESSED, NOTARIZED, AND USED RIGHT

Some legal documents to be valid need to be "witnessed", which is someone watching the person doing the form sign and then the witness signs it too. Some documents need to be "notarized" where a person who is a "notary" sees a page signed and uses an ink stamp and signs too. A person who is a notary (also called a "notary public") are at some banks, brokers, insurance agents, courts, law firms, mail-copy stores, and libraries.

Many people first use a phonebook to find a notary willing to help. The words "subscribe" and "execute" means a person signed a document, and "acknowledgment" means a person said a signature was theirs. If a person signs a document in a foreign language it is usually still binding. In a form the word "respectively" means "in the order just stated". When filling out a form except for signatures the other parts can usually be done in pencil and filled in by anyone. Later people often try to keep the original pages and only hand out copies. Some people have everyone sign multiple copies to have many copies with ink signatures.

SOME LESS COMMON OR LESS USEFUL FORMS ARE NOT IN THIS BOOK

This book skips some possible but less common or less useful legal documents.

- A "Codicil" can modify or add to a Will but it is easier and legally safer to just rewrite the whole Will.
- Some people do a "Pet Trust" to help a pet, but it's easier to just give money in Will to person given a pet.
- Some people do a "Revocable Living Trust" so a Trust entity with a Trustee holds property or money during their life, usually done to after death have faster transfer of things and to avoid small delays, costs, or work by others (by "avoiding probate"). But this is rare as it may require moving most of a person's things to a Trust causing maybe years of hassle, mostly to avoid later small work for people happy to be getting things.
- "Childrens Trust" papers can be done so upon a death a Trust gets things for a minor child to manage till 18, but this is rarely done due to possible costs and hassles and since it rarely matters (as this book explains).
- Though separate forms exist usually organ donation in handled in drivers license or state ID paperwork.
- Kentucky law, unlike many states, does <u>not</u> officially let a short list or memo add small gifts to a Will.

NO FEDERAL, KENTUCKY, OR OTHER TAX IS USUALLY OWED AT A DEATH

Usually no tax is owed due to a death, including no inheritance, estate, death, or similar taxes at all. <u>At the federal level, the "Federal Estate And Gift Tax" is only owed if a tax credit is used up that covers $13.99 million per person in 2025</u> and later, and this amount will increase each year to adjust for inflation. There is a <u>Kentucky inheritance tax but it does not tax gifts and transfers to close family</u> in "Class A" which is any spouse, parent, child (adopted or stepchild too), grandchild, and full or half brother or sister. More distant family and non-relatives are taxed on amounts over $1000 at rates from 4-16%, and some lawyers say this is usually 10% on average (so not very high). Basically if a person plans to have money and property go to close family after their death then usually no state tax is owed. <u>A few states may tax things there if the owner dies, but they often don't tax things if the total is under $3 million</u> or so.

PROBABLY RE-DO DOCUMENTS IF DIVORCE, MARRY, HAVE CHILD, OR MOVE

Divorcing, marrying, having a new child, or moving to a new state can have big legal effects, and if any of these events occur it is recommended people do a new Will and other Estate Planning papers soon. To help most states say a Will from another state is still valid if people move but this is not always certain.

"HELPFUL INFORMATION" FORM CAN TELL FAMILY AND FRIENDS THINGS

Often people do a "Helpful Information" form that some financial planners, lawyers, and banks suggest so family and friends after a death know things. Often people staple records or lists to this. <u>See next pages</u>.

ESTATE PLANNING HELPFUL INFORMATION

For more space attach copies of form or blank pages. Keep pages by Will or other place for Executor or family.

1. Personal Information (Name, Birthdate, Social Security number, special family details, other):

2. Real estate, vehicles, and other major tangible property (especially if people may not find them):

3. Non-tangible assets like stocks, accounts, investments, loans owed you, and business interests:

4. Possible income or insurance like pensions, retirement, disability, insurance, or contracts:

5. Debts owed by you like credit card, loan, student loan, mortgage, car loans, and accounts payable:

6. Names and information of professionals used (attorneys, accountants, brokers, doctors, others):

7. Computer passwords and helpful files, document places, and safes or safe-deposit boxes code/key:

8. Other helpful things, wishes for funeral, special requests, and last messages to family and friends:

CHAPTER 2
LEGAL TERMS AND BASIC PROPERTY LAW

THERE ARE BASIC LEGAL TERMS AND IDEAS IN ESTATE PLANNING

Some legal words and ideas are basic to Estate Planning.

■ "Estate Planning" is about people doing legal documents to control things if later absent, sick, or dead. After a document is done people are mostly free to sell or transfer property, instruct doctors, or change forms.

■ A "person doing a legal document" and "doing a form" means the form is for and affects that person.

■ "Probate" is a legal process to do things after someone's death like transfer property, handle creditors, and authorize a Guardian. Due to changes in the law probate is now often informal, faster, and less costly.

■ A "Will" or "will" (this book uses upper case "W") is a legal document done to control issues after death. The phrase "Last Will And Testament" is used since a "Testament" document use to be done alongside a Will.

■ A person doing a Will is called "Testator" or "Will maker". Before about the year 2000 a woman Testator was called a "Testatrix" and woman Executor called an "Executrix" but this is no longer often said or written.

■ If no valid Will is done a person is "intestate" and then a dead person's property and money is transferred to a spouse, children, and family as intestate law says. Some people a fine with this. This is covered later.

■ A person who died is called the "decedent" or "deceased". A person getting a Will gift is called a "recipient", "beneficiary", or "heir" if related (they "inherit"). "Survive" or "surviving" is to be alive after someone else died. The term "descendants" or "issue" usually means a person's children and grandchildren.

■ A person named in a Will to handle things after someone's death is called an "Executor", but if a judge has to pick someone they are called an "Administrator". The new term "Personal Representative" covers both these things and this new term is now commonly used in Wills in Kentucky and many states.

■ Legally property is: 1) "real property" which is land and buildings ("real estate"), 2) "fixtures" which are things tied to real property (like fences, carpets, and wired-in appliances), or 3) "personal property" which is everything else (like household items, clothes, tools, cars, jewelry, art, moneys, accounts, and stocks),

■ A person under 18 is usually called a "minor" and often a parent or guardian helps them do things. A minor or other person not reasonably able to make wise decisions lacks "capacity" and is "incapacitated".

■ A document giving power to someone is often called a "Power of Attorney" where the "Principal" gives power to someone called the "Agent" or "Attorney-in-Fact" (but they needn't be a real attorney or a lawyer).

■ State law is the "Kentucky Revised States" (revised means updated). A law is a "section" or "statute" shown by the "§" symbol. An example of how to refer to a law is: "Kentucky Revised Statutes § 395.455". A legal form written by the state into the law for people to find and use if wanted is called a "statutory form". Wills in Kentucky usually involve the local District Court in its Probate division.

ESTATE MEANS PROPERTY OF DECEDENT AND ENTITY HOLDING THINGS

The "estate" or "probate estate" means <u>all property and money of a dead person</u> that at death or soon after didn't automatically legally go to new owners. Estate is also the <u>name for a temporary entity run by an Executor to do things after a death</u> (it's like a small corporation, e.g., "Estate of John Alan Smith").

PERSON CAN ONLY GIFT IN WILL WHAT THEY OWN AT DEATH

A person can often only gift by Will things they own at death, <u>so people should research what they own</u>. Basically, by law a person usually owns all they earn as wages and salary, owns their share of income and profit tied to property they own, and owns or partly owns any things their money buys or improves. And for property with "title" documents (real estate or vehicles) or where there is a "listed owner" (like accounts) the named persons are usually the legal owners unless evidence shows special circumstances. If people don't keep track of how much of their money is in an account shared with a spouse, then the account may be seen as jointly owned 50/50. Note, after doing a Will a person can sell stuff, make gifts, or transfer things, so <u>people should consider if they later transferred or lost property they named in a Will gift</u>.

NON-PROBATE TRANSFERS THAT HAPPEN AUTOMATICALLY IGNORE WILL

It is vital to be aware <u>some money or property of a person who dies may automatically transfer on death</u> or soon after to new owners <u>if certain arrangements were made earlier</u>. This is called "non-probate property". Such things transfer as arranged even if a Will names the same items in some Will gifts.

Examples are: a) a "designated beneficiary" form was done to name people to get an investment or account, b) transfer-on-death accounts were used, and c) real property is held by 2 people as "joint tenants with survivorship" or similar so at a death the surviving person gets things. Also, usually property in a Trust will ignore a Will and transfer as Trust papers say to. Life insurance usually goes to the named beneficiary.

Trying to do non-probate transfers for all things is called "avoiding probate", but few people try this since it can cause years of hassle, benefits are small, and often some thing is missed. <u>When doing a Will people should consider non-probate transfers that will occur automatically at a death and consider what will be left</u>.

THINGS OWNED IN SPECIAL WAYS MAY LIMIT GIFTING IN WILL

A person should consider if they own real estate or other property in special ownership ways which may limit gifting by Will. Laws vary in different states but <u>some common special ways of ownership are</u>:

- "joint tenant with right of survivorship" or similar legal options may be used in papers, so at a death property goes automatically to other named owners despite what a Will says (this is often how spouses hold a home);
- papers say a "life estate" exists, so then if someone dies the other people in papers the get a thing; and
- "Trust property" occurs if paperwork made a Trust entity and then property was transferred into it or this is set to occur, so then the Trust papers control where things put in the Trust go after someone's death.

Simple "joint ownership" with many owners can occur if people do joint papers, all agree to it, buy with joint funds, or if a gift was to many people. Wills <u>can</u> gift joint property, like "I give my half of boat to Ed Hu".

CHAPTER 3
WILL BASICS

A WILL LETS A PERSON CONTROL THINGS AFTER THEIR DEATH

A Will is a legal document done by a person to control some things after their death. A person doing a Will is called the "Testator" or "Will maker". In Kentucky a Testator <u>when signing</u> a Will must be at least age 18, of sound mind (rational with sufficient memory), and not be under duress (unfair pressure or threat).

KEEP SIGNED WILL IN SAFE PLACE IT CAN BE FOUND AFTER A DEATH

A Will should be kept so it can be found within days of a death, like in a desk, drawer, safe, with a person, or (less often) a bank safe deposit box. Someone can be told how to find a Will. Most counties in Kentucky no longer let a person file a Will early during person's life for safekeeping with the county clerk.

A WILL USUALLY IS SIGNED WITH 2 WITNESSES

A WILL TO BE VALID USUALLY MUST BE SIGNED WITH 2 WITNESSES

To be a Will the words on a page must show it is a Will and then a person must usually <u>sign in front of at least 2 persons</u> acting as witnesses who then sign too. A Will just spoken on a video or audio recording usually has no legal effect. <u>Some people modify a Will to have 3 or 4 witnesses in case this may later help</u>. As this book later says if a Will is all handwritten then the 2 witnesses may not be legally needed.

WITNESSES SHOULD BE AT LEAST AGE 18 AND NOT GETTING WILL GIFTS

The witnesses to a Will signing can be anyone at least age 18, but preferably not old or living far away. In Kentucky if a person or their spouse are getting a Will gift then the person <u>can</u> be a witness but the gifts are void and canceled except close family can get up to amount "intestate law" gives them without a Will. Most lawyers use "disinterested" witnesses not getting Will gifts. Also, most lawyers try to not use witnesses named in a Will as Executor as Guardian. Often used as a witness is a friend, strangers, or distant family.

TESTATOR AND 2 WITNESSES SIGN THE WILL WHEN TOGETHER IN 1 ROOM

A person doing a Will usually signs with 2 or more witnesses who also sign while all are in 1 room and see others sign. A Testator or witness should <u>use their full legal name</u> unless they dislike and rarely use it. People showing others an ID is common but not required. Witnesses only read the 1 paragraph they sign. Also, often a Will has a witness print their name and address. But a Testator need not initial the Will pages. <u>Witnesses usually should be told by someone the document is a Will</u>. Though not required often a Testator says a thing like: "My name is _____ and this is my Will I do voluntarily and ask you 2 people to witness the signing". Some Testators chat with witnesses more about a Will to help show they know what they're doing.

CANCELING OLD WILLS IS USUALLY NOT A PROBLEM

So a new Will is followed old Wills should be canceled ("revoked"). To do this a new Will in the first part usually says old Wills are revoked. Or people can revoke a Will by marking it, like with "void" or a giant "X". Usually crossing out just part of a Will has no effect. Revoking a Will usually doesn't bring back an earlier Will.

OFTEN AT START OF WILL A PERSON NAMES ANY SPOUSE AND CHILDREN

Many Wills start with a place for a Testator to name any current living spouse and children of any age. Natural and adopted children should be put here including any born outside of marriage, but no stepchildren. People without this family can skip this or just write "none". Not doing this may invalidate a Will by indicating a person is mentally unfit, or let a spouse or child not listed ask a judge to give them part or everything by saying a Testator just forgot them. After listing people in a Will a Testator is mostly free to give them nothing.

WILLS SAY PEOPLE MAY LATER DO INFORMAL PROBATE AND SKIP BOND

Most Wills say after a death the family and friends may do "informal probate" which can avoid costs and delays. Informal probate often is done with just 1 court hearing and often is completed in well under 1 year. Also, most Wills helpfully say no "bond" or "surety" is required for any Executor, Guardian, or similar person. A bond is insurance from a company to insure against misconduct. A Testator usually doesn't want a bond since the persons Testator names are trusted and them later needing a bond will cost the estate money.

A WILL NAMES AN EXECUTOR TO DO THINGS AFTER DEATH

A WILL NAMES SOMEONE TO BE EXECUTOR TO DO THINGS AFTER A DEATH

Usually a Will names someone as "Executor" to act after a death. The law gives Executors many helpful legal powers, like to handle debts, find and collect and give new owners property and money, and do probate If a Will fails to name an Executor a judge can pick someone, but family may argue about who to suggest. An Executor is not expected to pay the dead person's debts and funeral costs with the Executor's own money and property. Note, the term "Personal Representative" and not Executor is often used in Kentucky for a person doing this job after a death, and these are similar terms. Will gifts can go to an Executor.

EXECUTOR CAN BE PAID AND ESTATE PAYS FOR EXECUTOR'S EXPENSES

State law says an Executor can ask to be paid for their work. Kentucky law says pay usually should be under 5% the value of property in the estate (excluding real property not sold) plus 5% of income collected. Pay for an Executor may help them get something even if there are large debts. But often Executors later skip asking for pay to not owe income tax and to leave more resources to later carry out Will gifts. But some people modify a Will to say the Executor should get no pay or less pay. Costs any Executor has like for insurance, utilities, repairs, funeral, mortgage, security, accountants, attorneys, and probate costs are paid for with money or property of the estate. A lawyer hired is usually paid what they and Executor agree on.

EXECUTOR MUST BE AT LEAST 18 AND SECOND PERSON RARELY IS NEEDED

In Kentucky a person must be at least 18 to be Executor. They must be a state resident unless related to Testator by blood, adoption, marriage, or spouse of such a person. Kentucky Revised Statutes § 395.005. In Kentucky an Executor can have a criminal record but a judge may later block a person who seems very unsuitable. Naming 2 people to be Executor at the same time is rare due to risk of arguments or delays, and since any 1 person named is trusted. People can name a 2nd fallback person to be Executor if needed but most skip this because it is rarely needed and a judge can always pick someone. To add such a 2nd person a Will can say: "or if they're reasonably unable to serve I name _____ to serve".

CHAPTER 4
WILL GIFTS INCLUDING RESIDUE CLAUSE

MAIN USE OF A WILL IS TO WRITE GIFTS TO HAPPEN AFTER DEATH
Most people use a Will mainly to legally say what happens to their property and money after their death, usually by writing down various Will gifts to occur when they die. Verbal and even writings about this are not usually valid if not in a written Will. A Will can control property acquired after it was signed. The end of this chapter covers "intestate law" which says where a person's things go at death if no valid Will handles this.

GIFTING IN A WILL USING SIMPLE WORDS OFTEN IS BEST
Making gifts in a Will using simple words is often best, using words like "I give to" and "I gift to". This is legally fine and avoids confusing legal words like "bequest", "devise", and "legacy" which few people know.

A PERSON IS MOSTLY FREE TO GIFT THEIR THINGS AS WANTED
A person is mostly free to give at death their money and property as they want. But creditors a decedent owed money, a spouse, and minor children under age 18 may have some rights which this book later covers.

IN WILL CAN DO SPECIFIC GIFTS TO GIFT PARTICULAR PROPERTY
Most Wills have "specific gifts" to gift <u>particular things</u>. Specific gifts can be any property, like "I give boat to Ed Blom" and "I give UBank account #84553873 to Sue Wu". If a gift is not clear the law assumes all of a kind of thing is given, like "I give jewelry to Ann Po" means <u>all</u> jewelry. But gifting specific property can have surprises like value of items can change, or a Will gift may later fail to occur if property is not owned at death.

IN WILL CAN DO GENERAL GIFTS LIKE OF MONEY
Wills can do "general gifts" where what is gifted is not particular property but can be flexibly chosen, like "I give 1 of my 3 cars to Ed Po" which lets an Executor pick which car. The usual general gift is money, like "I give $5 to Ed Hu". Money gifts are easy to write, let equal gifts be made, and are legally safer for many reasons. To carry out money gifts an Executor usually uses accounts or sells some property in the estate.

GIFTS IN WILL CAN GO TO A GROUP OR CLASS OF PEOPLE
To save work a Will gift can go to a group or class of people like certain family <u>if who is meant is later easy to determine</u>. People can say roughly how <u>much in total</u> is gifted to be clearer. Examples are: "I give $10 to each person in my 2018 bowling team" and "I give $10 to each of my grandkids so this is about $100 in total."

PROPERTY OR MONEY IN A JOINT GIFT GOES TO MULTIPLE PEOPLE
The same property or money can go to many people to each get a part, and this is called a "joint gift". For example, "I give boat and all hats to Ann Baxter and Mary Ann Swanson" means each person owns part of every item. People later can split things by agreement or an Executor can decide how to divide items. If a person in a joint gift has died their part usually is left to transfer under a Residue Clause.

RESIDUE CLAUSE IS CATCH-ALL THAT HELPFULLY GIFTS ANYTHING LEFT

This chapter later covers how a Residue Clause at a Will's end gifts property or money not already gifted. Sometimes this goes to a person or their "lineal descendants per stirpes" which means among their children and grandchildren with a equal share going to each branch of their family (this is explained later in this book).

CAN LEAVE SOME WILL GIFT AREAS BLANK OR WRITE TO SAY SKIP GIFTS

A person can choose to not use some gifts areas in a Will legal form, like by just leaving areas blank, writing things like "SKIPPED" or "NONE", or using a computer to delete some gift lines. Judges and others usually do not care about neatness or empty spaces in Wills, and will follow whatever parts are filled in.

FAMILIES MAY LET PEOPLE TAKE ITEMS BUT LISTS ARE NOT FULLY LEGAL

Many families let people take items <u>unofficially</u> in ways a person said, showed by stickers, or put on notes. If anyone officially objects a judge will have a Will and law be fully followed, but later people can voluntarily retransfer items. Note, Kentucky unlike some states does <u>not</u> officially let a list or memo add gifts to a Will.

LATER DIVORCE OR MURDER CANCELS WILL GIFTS TO THE ACTING PERSON

If a person divorces or murders a Testator then by state law usually all Will gifts to them are cancelled.

CONDITIONS ON WILL GIFTS ARE RARE DUE TO POSSIBLE PROBLEMS

Putting conditions on a gift, like "I give Ann Poe $90 if she graduates college", can cause problems like years of delay, risk of lawsuits, and big attorney's fees. Due to all this conditions are rarely put on Will gifts.

MOST WILLS HAVE A MISCELLANEOUS PART WITH HELPFUL LANGUAGE

Most Wills have a "Miscellaneous" page with legal language that might help avoid later legal problems.

INTESTATE LAW COVERS PROPERTY OR MONEY NOT HANDLED BY WILL

State "intestate law" says where property and money goes if no valid Will was done before person died (except for certain rights of spouses, family, and creditors). Intestacy laws often say half and sometimes all goes to any surviving spouse (if any), then half or any remainder goes to decedent's children (or if dead their own child gets that share), then next closest family, and then to the state. <u>Many people are happy with intestate law and intentionally die with no Will</u>, but many people do a Will to get the exact distribution wanted and other reasons. For intestate law a fully adopted child counts but not foster-child or step-child. <u>Kentucky intestate law is a bit unusual</u> and people not doing a Will to control things may want to do research Kentucky intestate law.

RESIDUE CLAUSE GIFTING ANYTHING LEFT IS MAIN WAY TO GIFT THINGS

THE RESIDUE CLAUSE IS A CATCH-ALL THAT GIFTS ANYTHING LEFT

Most Wills by the end have a Residue Clause to give property or money left in a person's estate not gifted earlier in a Will or used other ways. All that is left this way is called the "Residue". Many people let this clause handle most things. This avoids all need to list and describe property and money and also has less legal risk.

USUAL RESIDUE CLAUSE HAS 2 PARTS

A short 2 part Residue Clause is usual and is used in this book's Will forms, and it has:

1) a 1st space to name persons to get things if they survive the Testator (many name a spouse or closest family here), and if several people are named here but only some survive the survivors split things, and

2) a 2nd space to name persons to get things if all in the 1st space don't survive (many people name next closest family or friends here), and if a person in the 2nd space has died their descendants get their share.

EXAMPLE OF 2 PART RESIDUE CLAUSE:

"RESIDUE CLAUSE: The rest, residue, and remainder of my estate, and anything else, I give to:

 a) to   Jay Doe my husband   who survive me and with persons just named who survive me taking the share of non-survivors, then if anything remains

 b) to   Sam Doe, Ann Wu, and Pam Ax   and if any of those just named do not survive me their part goes to their lineal descendants per stirpes."

In this example things may go to "descendants" so among a person's children and grandchildren, and things are divided "per stirpes" which means equal among family branches. In this example if Jay Doe has survived he gets everything. If he has died and also Sam Doe has died but he left 2 children then, legally, Sam's 2 children split the 1/3 share of his (so get 1/6 each) and the other 2 persons in 2nd part (Ann Wu and Pam Ax) get 1/3 each. Usually the first people named in the clause won't die so gets things.

PEOPLE CAN PUT SAME THING IN PARTS, OR SKIP PART, OR USE PERCENTAGE

Some people put the same 1 person in both parts of a Residue Clause, to fully ensure that 1 person or if they later die their descendants will get things. Or a person with no spouse may skip the Residue Clause 1st part and in the 2nd part put their children (including any who died who had a child), so all branches of a family get an equal share. *See Appendix.* Many people use percentages in the Residue Clause. *See Appendix.*

SOME PEOPLE CHANGE A RESIDUE CLAUSE TO HAVE 1 PART

Some people change a Residue Clause to have just 1 part since this can gift more equally and be easier to understand. *See example in Appendix.* For example a Residue Clause can be made to say:

"The rest, residue, and remainder of my estate, and anything else, I give to _____ who survive me and if any of those just named do not survive me their part goes to their lineal descendants per stirpes."

MUST SUFFICIENTLY DESCRIBE NAMES AND PROPERTY IN A WILL

PUTTING NAMES OF PEOPLE OR GROUPS IN A WILL IS FAIRLY EASY

Putting names in a Will is fairly easy. <u>Later a judge or Executor assume a person putting names in a Will meant to gift to people they know, so common names are OK unless 2 friends or family use the same name</u>. Details can help if names won't be recognized or to be friendly, like "I give $5 to my nurse Sue Smith" and "I give $5 to loyal pal Ed Dutton". If people mostly used a nickname "also known as" or "a/k/a" may help, like "I give $5 to Dan Smith a/k/a Big Red". Gifts can go to a charity, a government, or a group, like "I give $8 to Goodwill Charities, "I give $8 to the Trigg County Library in Kentucky", and "I give $8 to Holy Trinity Church of Dallas, Texas". People sometimes phone to learn a charity's or organization's official name.

PUTTING DESCRIPTIONS OF ITEMS IN WILL GIFTS IS FAIRLY EASY

Describing items in gifts is fairly easy. <u>Later a judge or Executor assume a person in a Will meant to gift items they own, and rarely do people own similar things so there is later confusion</u>. Often OK is doing gifts with simple words like: "I give ax to Ed Wu" and "I give big table to Jed Fox". It's OK to gift by category or a list, like: "I give tools to Sam Lee" and "I give cow, van, and harp to Sue Hill". For financial items plain words can be used, like "I give bank accounts and stocks to Ann Bima", or details can be used, like: "I give Wells Fargo bank account ending 8714 to Tom Hud". <u>Gifting using a location is riskier</u> as judges will ignore a Will gift if it seems items were placed to affect gifting and for no "independently significant" life reason. So, "I give Ed Po items in my desk and safe" a judge might not follow, but "I give Ed Po hats at cabin" likely is OK.

DESCRIBING REAL PROPERTY IS HARD IF NOT USING RESIDUE OR TITLE

Gifting real property (real estate) and fixtures (things tied to real property like fences, furnaces, and wiring) at death can be hard to do right and the legally safer way to do this is:

a) <u>do nothing specific so it's handled by a Will residue clause</u>, or b) <u>have a lawyer or other person put names in a deed or other document for the real property</u> so then named persons legally get it when the owner dies.

Gifting real property at death a few other ways is legally harder. Helpfully a gift of real property <u>using a location</u> by law gifts <u>all land, buildings, and fixtures located there</u> with no need to list out what's there.

It is possible to <u>gift real property at a particular address with very plain words</u>, like a house, fixtures, and land can be fully given by something like: "I give 86 Maxwell Street, Frankfort, Kentucky, to Sue Ann Brown".

People can do a <u>blanket gift</u> giving all of a kind of property, like, "I give all real property and fixtures in Kenton County, Kentucky to Ann Ivy Hill" or "I give all real property and fixtures of mine to Eric Paul Carlson".

Giving real property in a Will using a "legal description" is how some lawyers do it, but this can be hard to do. If using a legal description people must write without mistakes <u>the full legal description of maybe many lines</u> into a Will with no abbreviation at all. A legal description might be found on a deed or on mortgage papers. Legal descriptions may refer to a "lot" or "blocks" on a map which is recorded in land records of a county, or it may refer to a path around the land borders with various angles, distances, and iron stakes.

OPTIONS EXIST TO HANDLE RARE CASE PERSON IN A WILL GIFT DIES

PERSON IN WILL GIFT USUALLY MUST SURVIVE OR GIFT DOES NOT OCCUR

Though rarely an issue, many Wills like this book's Will forms say a person named in a Will gift must survive (live past) the Testator or the gift will not later occur unless gift language specifically says different. If survival isn't required like this then what occurs can be unclear (for many reasons like certain state laws). Most people if they see a person in a gift has died just re-do a Will or trust a Residue Clause to handle it.

SOME PEOPLE ADD "ALTERNATE BENEFICIARY" MAYBE FOR SPECIAL ITEMS

Some people to handle if a person named in a Will gift dies maybe put for special items an alternate beneficiary, like for example: "I give oak table to Ed Wu but if they don't survive me to Ben Fox".

IF PERSON IN WILL GIFT DIES IT CAN GO TO "LINEAL DESCENDANTS"

A Will gift can say it goes to a person but if they don't survive the Testator then say the gift goes to the person's "lineal descendants". Descendants are a person's children and grandchildren. Also, the term "per stirpes" is often used to say to give to each family branch equally. An example shows how this works:

A Will may say: "All clothes to Sue Wu but if they don't survive to their lineal descendants per stirpes", and this means if Sue Wu has died and her son Ken Wu is living and her other son Ben Wu has died but left 2 children then, legally, by law Ken Wu himself gets 50% and Ben Wu's 2 children each get 25%.

HELPFUL LAWS OFTEN REQUIRE PERSON SURVIVE 120 HOURS TO GET GIFT

Laws in most states say a person dying within 120 hours of someone is seen as having died earlier, so often a Will gift to them is ignored. This avoids legal problems like need to know exact time of death and, also, having an item go through many probate legal cases over years.

CHAPTER 5
DEBT, FAMILY, SPOUSE, HOMESTEAD, AND CHILD ISSUES

THIS CHAPTER COVERS CERTAIN ISSUES THAT SOME PEOPLE CAN SKIP
This chapter covers debt, family, spouse, homestead, and child issues, and some people can skip parts.

DEBT ISSUES

PAYING DECEDENT'S DEBTS MAY USE UP RESOURCES AND REDUCE GIFTS
If a person who dies (a decedent) had debts then creditors owed may ask a judge to be paid from the decedent's money or property <u>before</u> Will gifts and certain transfers occur. How debts are paid is set by state law and a Will need not cover this. Funds to pay debts comes from decedent's money and property so may affect (in order) the Will Residue, Will general gifts, Will specific gifts, and non-probate transfers. Probate, health care, taxes, and funeral costs by law have some priority to be paid first. For various reasons often not all creditors owed are ever paid. <u>People should consider how paying debts may use up money or property of a decedent, leaving less to carry out Will gifts</u>. Note, a spouse and family usually aren't liable for decedent's debts unless they actually guaranteed or co-signed. People who want can do research.

SECURED DEBTS LIKE MORTGAGE OR VEHICLE LIEN ARE NOT PAID OFF
Laws in most states say <u>do not pay off any secured debts on property of a decedent</u> like a house mortgage or vehicle lien even if other debts are paid by Executor or in probate. This avoids using up estate resources on paying these often big debts. All this book's Will forms clearly say do not usually pay off any secured debts. But if a Testator wants they can 1) put in a Will an order to pay (like, "Executor pay off the house mortgage"), or 2) gift enough money to pay off a secured debt like a mortgage or lien to the person getting the property. Most banks let the new owners after a death keep paying monthly any secured debt like a mortgage or lien. People who want can do research.

FAMILY ISSUES

FAMILY RIGHTS MAY BE USED TO GET FAMILY THINGS BEFORE DEBTS
Many states have "Family Rights" a decedent's surviving spouse or children can use, and this may help let them get things <u>before most debts of decedent are paid</u> and even <u>before Will gifts are ever carried out</u>. State law varies but this can include an "Exempt Property" right to some of decedent's household items and vehicles to use to live, like $20,000 of this. This can include a "Family Allowance" right to get some money to live on for a year or so from the decedent's property and money. This can include the right to use a "Small Estate Affidavit" to quickly get a spouse or children most things if a decedent didn't leave much overall, like under $50,000 of things. <u>Kentucky law partly has all these rights</u>, and most people with a spouse or children accept their family has rights to get some things. <u>So family don't cause legal trouble by using these rights often a person with family in some way usually gives over 50% of their things and any family dwelling they own to any spouse or small children</u>. People who want can do research.

SPOUSE ISSUES

KENTUCKY USES SEPARATE PROPERTY LAW FOR SPOUSES

Kentucky like most states not in the West U.S. uses the Separate Property Law system that says any married person mostly owns their money and property separately and not jointly shared with a spouse. Due to this a married person here is often free to sell during life or gift by Will most their property and money and not involve a spouse. But joint ownership by 2 spouses and not separate ownership can arise in other ways, like by agreement, both spouses paying part of the purchase price, if a gift was to both spouses, or if paperwork calls it joint.

COMMUNITY PROPERTY LAW APPLIES IN OTHER STATES FOR SPOUSES

There are 9 states mostly in the West U.S.A. that use "Community Property" law for married people (Arizona, California, Louisiana, Idaho, Nevada, New Mexico, Texas, Washington, and also Wisconsin). This law says if a married person lives in these states most property or money gotten is usually owned 50/50 by spouses as "Community Property" if it relates to activities during marriage (like from labor or wages, major physical or mental effort, or active management of a business) or if bought or improved with other Community Property. Most people avoid these issues unless recently moving to or from these states.

SPOUSE CAN GET SHARE INSTEAD OF FOLLOWING WILL

In most states a spouse if unhappy with what a Will and other transfers may give them has options, and often they have a right for a spouse to choose a share of a dead spouse's property and money rather than take what a Will says. Many states let a spouse choose (elect) an "Elective Share" like half of decedent's things, or some states give a percentage like 15% and rising with years of marriage to 50% after 15 years. In some cases this can cover things decedent gave away or things controlled but not owned. Kentucky has a related but unique system to help a surviving spouse, and this involves the concept of "dower and curtesy" which let a spouse choose a share of certain valuable property of the dead spouse. To avoid these issues both spouses would have to sign from a lawyer a long pre-nuptial or post-nuptial agreement which is rare. Usually to avoid a spouse wanting to use these complex rights most married people in a Will and other ways give over 1/2 of their money and property to any spouse. People who want can do research.

HOMESTEAD ISSUES

In many states a surviving spouse or children till age 18 have under a "Homestead Law" some right to get (or just stay in for years) the house or mobile home the family or decedent lived in if owned by a decedent. Kentucky partly has these rights, and most people with a spouse or children accept family may have some rights to their home. Kentucky "quarantine" law also may let a spouse or children stay. Also, an unhappy spouse may sue claiming promises were made, like: "He said I get the house if I stayed during his illness". If these rights are used it may interfere with other things. Due to this often a person gives property used as a home to family by Will or other way so they don't bother with these rights. People who want can do research.

CHILD ISSUES

WILL CAN NAME A PERSON TO GIVE PERSONAL CARE FOR ANY YOUNG CHILD

If a parent dies with a child under age 18 then any other natural or adopted parent (but not a step-parent) usually automatically gets control of the child's personal care (including health care, school, and home issues). This won't occur only if the other parent will be unavailable a long time or is proven unfit in court which is rare. But just in case it's ever needed (like later both parents die) a Will often names a healthy willing relative or friend as "Guardian" to if needed give this care for a child. Some states call this a "Guardian Of The Person".

WILL CAN NAME A PERSON TO MANAGE CHILD'S PROPERTY AND MONEY

Since a child until age 18 can't legally easily control property and money a Will often names a person to have the job of managing property and money a child has or may get. This person decides each year how to use property and money on a child's needs (like on school, health care, and living costs) and then usually at age 18 anything left then goes to the child. A person paying things for a child can later ask to be paid back. In Kentucky usually a Guardian giving personal care for a child is given power to manage their property and money, and the term used is usually still just Guardian. Some states call this a "Guardian Of The Estate". As a nice 2nd option to avoid legal work and costs most Wills say an Executor may name a person including themselves as "Custodian" to handle a child's property and money under the Uniform Transfers To Minors Act.

MOST WILLS NAME 1 PERSON TO CARE FOR CHILD AND THEIR PROPERTY

This book's Will forms and most parents name the same 1 person to care for a child and also manage a child's property and money. In Kentucky if power over property and money is not given to a Guardian who is also giving personal care to a child then the person managing property and money is called a "Conservator". A Will can be changed to name different people for the 2 jobs, but this is rarely worth it since parents dying is rare, rarely do children get much, a person caring for children usually if smart enough to handle finances, and naming different people can lead to arguments and lawsuits.

PERSON TO HELP A CHILD MUST BE AT LEAST 18

To serve in these jobs a person must be at least 18 and usually have no record of bad crime, committing abuse, or fraud. A person needn't be a state resident. A judge may later block a person who seems too unsuitable. The choice by the last living parent is usually followed unless it won't be best for a child. If no Will picks a person for a position or they're unavailable a judge can pick someone, but family may argue and fight about who to suggest. Naming 2 people to act at the same time in the same position is rare since 2 persons may argue and any 1 person named is often smart enough to act alone. Sometimes the 2 people in a married couple are named for the same position but there can be problems if they later divorce or argue. Some Wills add a 2nd person to serve if the 1st person named is later not available, like: "or if they are later unable to serve I name ____ to serve"). But most people skip naming a fallback person since it is rarely needed, if a problem is seen a Will can be redone by a person, or a judge can always pick someone to serve.

NAMING PERSONS TO HELP CHILD RARELY MATTERS

A child under 18 having parents die is rare so parents shouldn't worry much about naming people to help. A good study looked at 72,240 people under age 18 and found only 2014 had lost 1 parent (so 2.78%) and only 97 had lost 2 parents (so a very small 0.13%). *Parent Mortality Census SIPP Paper #288.*

CHAPTER 6
BASIC IDEAS ABOUT HEALTH CARE FORMS

THERE ARE SOME BASIC IDEAS ABOUT HEALTH CARE FORMS
Some ideas help people understand health care forms.

■ By law people controls their own health care by telling medical personnel what they want unless they are "incapacitated" by insufficient ability to a) communicate verbally or by notes, b) be rational, or c) be conscious. Most people keep control of their own care till death or till no big treatment options remain, but some people worry they may be incapacitated a long time so want to do health care forms.

■ Legal documents that help control health care are usually called "Advanced Directives".

■ If an adult 18 or older becomes incapacitated the adult's closest family like spouse or adult child usually can make emergency decisions. But later they usually must then rush to a judge to get further power if no legal document gives them more power over health care.

■ In legal documents a person can be named to have control of health care if needed. This person is often called the "Health Care Agent", "Health Care Attorney-in-Fact", "Health Care Advocate", or a similar name.

■ In legal documents people can write medical instructions doctors, family, and other people must obey.

■ Parents even without legal documents mostly have full power over health care of children under age 18, and the only exception is teens have some freedom to pick their own family planning or gender related care.

■ Some married people do documents to give a spouse power over medical care if they are incapacitated. Some adults especially to age 25 do documents to give this power to parents. The young are less often sick.

■ Pain relief like pain drugs or comfort care is still given even if documents say to stop or limit other care.

■ Most people only do 1 legal document about health care that often names someone to control health care if needed and has a spot for basic instructions (this is sometimes called a "Health Care Power of Attorney").

■ For the rare times stopping health care seems more likely to matter (like due to extreme illness or old age):

-- most people do nothing special and trust family or Health Care Agent to wisely decide when to stop care (they can weigh many factors like pain, cost, likely difficulty of treatment, beliefs, and chances of recovery);

-- a few people do a serious document to say to stop most health care if <u>later</u> doctors think an incapacitated person has very bad health and more medical care likely won't help (sometimes this is called a "Living Will";

-- a few people do a serious document to say <u>starting immediately</u> to not give most medical care (often this is called a "Do-Not-Resuscitate" if about resuscitation, or called a "Physician's Order" if about many treatments).

CHAPTER 7
FORM 1: WILL (STANDARD)

FORM 1 IS A STANDARD WILL THAT IS FLEXIBLE BUT WITHOUT GUARDIANS

Form 1 is a flexible Will that lets a person control many things after their death. This form has no part about a Guardian so is for a person with no child under age 18. A person doing a Will is called a Testator. The term "Last Will And Testament" is often used since in the past a Testament page was done with a Will.

THIS FORM IS A WILL WITH SEVERAL PARTS

The form starts with lines for a person to put their name (a full legal name is best but not required) and place of main residence (most put a county but some put a city). The Will is still valid if people later move.

Paragraph 1, "Living Spouse And Children", is used to write names of any living spouse and living children (but not step-children) of any age (or if there are none skip this or maybe put "none"). This helps show a person is mentally fit enough to do a Will. Wrongly not listing someone may cause legal problems.

Paragraph 2, "Gifts", has many spaces to make some specific gifts of particular property or some general gifts like of money. People can delete, copy and paste to add more, or leave blank these gift lines.

Paragraph 3, "Residue", has a Residue Clause to say any property and money left after earlier Will parts and other transfers is to be distributed in the way a person wrote in the blank parts of this paragraph.

Paragraph 4, "Administration", names a person to be Personal Representative to do things after a person's death (in the past the term Executor was usually used in Kentucky for the person doing this).

Paragraph 5, "Miscellaneous", has paragraphs of legal language to help avoid certain legal issues.

Last is a paragraph for Testator to put the date and sign, and a paragraph for 2 witnesses to put the date, sign, and print the addresses they live at.

USUAL RESIDUE CLAUSE HAS 2 PLACES TO NAME PERSONS TO GET THINGS

In a Will "Residue Clause" anything left over after other Will parts is transferred as the clause directs. Many people use a Residue Clause to gift most their things. In this Will form's Residue Clause there is:

1) a 1st space to name 1 or more persons to get the Residue, and if any named here have died before the Will maker then other persons named here in this 1st space take the dead person's share, and

2) a 2nd space to name people to get things if all people named in the 1st space have died, and if any people named in the 2nd space have died their shares go to "lineal descendants" like their children.

People often put in the 1st space a spouse or closest family or friends, and in 2nd space next close people.

TESTATOR AND 2 WITNESSES WHILE TOGETHER SIGN WILL

This Will after being filled out (except bits intentionally left blank) must be signed by the person doing the Will (the "Testator") in front of at least 2 persons acting as witnesses at least age 18 who then also sign.

LAST WILL AND TESTAMENT

I, _____, of _____, Kentucky, do revoke all prior Wills and testamentary documents and do make, publish, and declare this as my Will. I am of sound mind and under no duress or undue influence and act voluntarily.

1. LIVING SPOUSE AND CHILDREN. To show I am mentally fit and have sufficient memory to do a Will I do say I now have the following living spouse and living children: _____
_____.

2. GIFTS. I give these gifts in this Will, but to get a gift in this section the recipient must survive me except as otherwise stated below.

I give _____ to _____.
I give _____ to _____.
I give _____ to _____.
I give _____ to _____.
I give _____ to _____.
I give _____ to _____.
I give _____ to _____.
I give _____ to _____.
I give _____ to _____.
I give _____ to _____.
I give _____ to _____.
I give _____ to _____.

3. RESIDUE. The rest, residue, and remainder of my estate, and anything else, I give:
   a) to _____ who survive me, and with persons just named who survive me taking the share of non-survivors, then if anything remains
   b) to _____ and if any of those just now named do not survive me their part goes to their lineal descendants per stirpes.

4. ADMINISTRATION. I name, nominate, and appoint _____
as Personal Representative including for me, my Will, and my estate.

5. MISCELLANEOUS. The following applies to this Will and generally.
   In this Will no part left unfilled is a mistake including spaces in the residue clause.
   The facts support and I want Kentucky law to apply to this Will and my estate.
   I order that my just debts, funeral and related expenses, and taxes be paid as soon after my death as practical but only those items my Personal Representative chooses to pay.
   Priority of Will gifts of the same type is based on the order they are made in this Will.
   The words give and gift also means a devise, bequest, grant, legacy, or similar.
   I am intentionally not providing by Will or other ways for some family, including I am not providing for some children of mine and also children of a deceased child of mine.
   If a Will gift reasonably mentions survival then survival is an absolute condition and anti-lapse laws or similar provisions have no effect and without survival the gift lapses. Unless a Will gift specifies otherwise if a Will gift goes to multiple recipients if any do not survive me the part to them lapses and instead goes to other surviving recipients.
   No earlier transfer reduces a Will gift unless I usually called it a loan or advancement.
   In this Will any gendered word includes all genders, and the singular includes the plural and vice versa, and they can mean a single person or many persons.
   Unless a Will specifically says otherwise a secured debt including a mortgage or lien shall not be paid off including by a Personal Representative or in probate, and a recipient of a Will gift of property takes it subject to debts. Also, no recipient of property who may lose it or who pays to keep it may have my estate or other people pay or do exoneration.
   If I somehow lost ownership of an item in a specific Will gift the gift is extinguished.
   I request and authorize any informal, summary, and quick probate or similar action. Any Personal Representative may act independently with no supervision of any court, including independent administration, and with no inventory, appraisal, or other action.
   I give any Personal Representative the a) fullest authority, discretion, and powers allowed by state law, b) power to lease, sell, mortgage, convey, or keep property including real property in a manner and time they deem helpful or proper, and c) authority to settle or pay claims or debts in the time and manner they choose. Any Personal Representative or other fiduciary shall have all powers and authorities that may be given by statute or common law in any jurisdiction they may act, including under Kentucky law.
   Any Guardian of any type, Conservator, Custodian, or other person managing a minor's property or money may use or invade the principal and sell property without court action.
   If context permits the terms Personal Representative and Executor and Administrator are interchangeable, Conservator and Guardian of the Estate and Guardian of Property and Custodian are interchangeable, and residue and residuary are interchangeable. Any such person may stand in the place of and have all powers like the others named here.

The residue includes lapsed or failed gifts, insurance paid to the estate, digital assets, inheritances owed me, and all I had power of appointment or testamentary disposition over.

Any Personal Representative may access, manage, delete, modify, transfer, and otherwise control any digital accounts and assets I had any interest in or power over.

Any Personal Representative, Executor, Administrator, Guardian of any type like for a person or estate, Conservator, Custodian, and any other fiduciary under this Will or otherwise shall qualify and serve without bond, surety, security, surety bond, or similar.

If evidence does not show it likely a person survived me by 120 hours (5 days) then for this Will and my estate they shall be deemed in all ways as having died before me.

A spouse using dower or curtesy rights may not get any gift or benefits of this Will.

Any Personal Representative may at any time transfer money or property of a minor under age 18 to a Custodian to act under the Kentucky Uniform Transfers to Minors Act or similar law anywhere, and may pick a person to be Custodian including themselves.

If part of this Will is by law invalid or unenforceable other provisions remain in effect.

TESTATOR

IN WITNESS WHEREOF, I, _____, the Testator, on the _____ day of _____, 20____, sign my name to this instrument and do hereby declare that I sign and execute this instrument willingly as my Will, that I execute it as my free and voluntary act for the purposes expressed in it, and that I am 18 years of age or older, of sound mind, and under no constraint or undue influence.

_____
Signature of Testator

WITNESSES

We, _____ and _____, the Witnesses, on the date indicated above, sign our names to this instrument, and do hereby declare that the Testator willingly signs and executes this instrument as the Will of the Testator, that each of us in the presence and hearing of the Testator and the other Witness who is signing hereby signs this Will to act as witnesses to the Testator's signing, and to the best of our knowledge the Testator is 18 years of age or older, of sound mind, and under no constraint or undue influence.

_____ _____
Signature of Witness #1   Address of Witness #1

_____ _____
Signature of Witness #2   Address of Witness #2

CHAPTER 8
FORM 2: WILL (GUARDIAN)

FORM 2 IS A WILL WITH GUARDIAN PART FOR PEOPLE WITH YOUNG CHILD

Form 2 is a Will with a Guardian part to be used by a person with a minor child under age 18. The term "Last Will And Testament" is often used since in the past a Testament was a document done with a Will.

FORM IS A WILL WITH SEVERAL PARTS INCLUDING A GUARDIAN PART

The form starts with lines for a person to put their name (a full legal name is best but not required) and place of main residence (most put a county but some put a city). The Will is still valid if people later move.

Paragraph 1, "Living Spouse And Children", is used to write names of any living spouse and living children (but not step-children) of any age (or if there are none skip this or maybe put "none"). This helps show a person is mentally fit enough to do a Will. Wrongly not listing someone may cause legal problems.

Paragraph 2, "Gifts", has many spaces to make some specific gifts of particular property or some general gifts like of money. People can delete, copy and paste to add more, or leave blank these gift lines.

Paragraph 3, "Residue", has a Residue Clause to say any property and money left after earlier Will parts and other transfers is to be distributed in the way a person wrote in the blank parts of this paragraph.

Paragraph 4, "Administration", names a person to be Personal Representative to do things after a person's death (in the past the term Executor was usually used in Kentucky for the person doing this).

<u>**Paragraph 5, "Guardian",** names a person to care for minor children under age 18 if needed (like if both parents die) and also a person to manage property and money of children</u>.

Paragraph 6, "Miscellaneous", has paragraphs of legal language to help avoid certain legal issues.

Last is a paragraph for Testator to put the date and sign, and a paragraph for 2 witnesses to put the date, sign, and print the addresses they live at.

USUAL RESIDUE CLAUSE HAS 2 PLACES TO NAME PERSONS TO GET THINGS

In a Will "Residue Clause" anything left over after other Will parts is transferred as the clause directs. Many people use a Residue Clause to gift most their things. In this Will form's Residue Clause there is:

1) a 1st space to name 1 or more persons to get the Residue, and if any named here have died before the Will maker then other persons named here in this 1st space take the dead person's share, and

2) a 2nd space to name people to get things if all people named in the 1st space have died, and if any people named in the 2nd space have died their shares go to "lineal descendants" like their children.

People often put in the 1st space a spouse or closest family or friends, and in 2nd space next close people.

TESTATOR AND 2 WITNESSES WHILE TOGETHER SIGN WILL

This Will after being filled out (except bits intentionally left blank) must be signed by the person doing the Will (the "Testator") in front of at least 2 persons acting as witnesses at least age 18 who then also sign.

LAST WILL AND TESTAMENT

I, _____, of _____, Kentucky, do revoke all prior Wills and testamentary documents and do make, publish, and declare this as my Will. I am of sound mind and under no duress or undue influence and act voluntarily.

1. LIVING SPOUSE AND CHILDREN. To show I am mentally fit and have sufficient memory to do a Will I do say I now have the following living spouse and living children:
_____
_____.

2. GIFTS. I give these gifts in this Will, but to get a gift in this section the recipient must survive me except as otherwise stated below.

I give _____ to _____.
I give _____ to _____.
I give _____ to _____.
I give _____ to _____.
I give _____ to _____.
I give _____ to _____.
I give _____ to _____.
I give _____ to _____.
I give _____ to _____.
I give _____ to _____.
I give _____ to _____.

3. RESIDUE. The rest, residue, and remainder of my estate, and anything else, I give:
  a) to _____ who survive me, and with persons just named who survive me taking the share of non-survivors, then if anything remains
  b) to _____ and if any of those just now named do not survive me their part goes to their lineal descendants per stirpes.

4. ADMINISTRATION. I name, nominate, and appoint _____ as Personal Representative including for me, my Will, and my estate.

5. GUARDIAN. I name _____ to be Guardian of any minor child of mine and to have care, authority, custody, and other control of them. The person just named above shall also act as Guardian in all matters involving any minor child's property, money, and estate and they shall have care, control, and power over these things (including as Conservator if this is helpful).

6. MISCELLANEOUS. The following applies to this Will and generally.

In this Will no part left unfilled is a mistake including spaces in the residue clause.

The facts support and I want Kentucky law to apply to this Will and my estate.

I order that my just debts, funeral and related expenses, and taxes be paid as soon after my death as practical but only those items my Personal Representative chooses to pay.

Priority of Will gifts of the same type is based on the order they are made in this Will.

The words give and gift also means a devise, bequest, grant, legacy, or similar.

I am intentionally not providing by Will or other ways for some family, including I am not providing for some children of mine and also children of a deceased child of mine.

If a Will gift reasonably mentions survival then survival is an absolute condition and anti-lapse laws or similar provisions have no effect and without survival the gift lapses. Unless a Will gift specifies otherwise if a Will gift goes to multiple recipients if any do not survive me the part to them lapses and instead goes to other surviving recipients.

No earlier transfer reduces a Will gift unless I usually called it a loan or advancement.

In this Will any gendered word includes all genders, and the singular includes the plural and vice versa, and they can mean a single person or many persons.

Unless a Will specifically says otherwise a secured debt including a mortgage or lien shall not be paid off including by a Personal Representative or in probate, and a recipient of a Will gift of property takes it subject to debts. Also, no recipient of property who may lose it or who pays to keep it may have my estate or other people pay or do exoneration.

If I somehow lost ownership of an item in a specific Will gift the gift is extinguished.

I request and authorize any informal, summary, and quick probate or similar action. Any Personal Representative may act independently with no supervision of any court, including independent administration, and with no inventory, appraisal, or other action.

I give any Personal Representative the a) fullest authority, discretion, and powers allowed by state law, b) power to lease, sell, mortgage, convey, or keep property including real property in a manner and time they deem helpful or proper, and c) authority to settle or pay claims or debts in the time and manner they choose. Any Personal Representative or other fiduciary shall have all powers and authorities that may be given by statute or common law in any jurisdiction they may act, including under Kentucky law.

Any Guardian of any type, Conservator, Custodian, or other person managing a minor's property or money may use or invade the principal and sell property without court action.

If context permits the terms Personal Representative and Executor and Administrator are interchangeable, Conservator and Guardian of the Estate and Guardian of Property and Custodian are interchangeable, and residue and residuary are interchangeable. Any such

person may stand in the place of and have all powers like the others named here.

The residue includes lapsed or failed gifts, insurance paid to the estate, digital assets, inheritances owed me, and all I had power of appointment or testamentary disposition over.

Any Personal Representative may access, manage, delete, modify, transfer, and otherwise control any digital accounts and assets I had any interest in or power over.

Any Personal Representative, Executor, Administrator, Guardian of any type like for a person or estate, Conservator, Custodian, and any other fiduciary under this Will or otherwise shall qualify and serve without bond, surety, security, surety bond, or similar.

If evidence does not show it likely a person survived me by 120 hours (5 days) then for this Will and my estate they shall be deemed in all ways as having died before me.

A spouse using dower or curtesy rights may not get any gift or benefits of this Will.

Any Personal Representative may at any time transfer money or property of a minor under age 18 to a Custodian to act under the Kentucky Uniform Transfers to Minors Act or similar law anywhere, and may pick a person to be Custodian including themselves.

If part of this Will is by law invalid or unenforceable other provisions remain in effect.

TESTATOR

IN WITNESS WHEREOF, I, _____, the Testator, on the _____ day of _____, 20____, sign my name to this instrument and do hereby declare that I sign and execute this instrument willingly as my Will, that I execute it as my free and voluntary act for the purposes expressed in it, and that I am 18 years of age or older, of sound mind, and under no constraint or undue influence.

_____
Signature of Testator

WITNESSES

We, _____ and _____, the Witnesses, on the date indicated above, sign our names to this instrument, and do hereby declare that the Testator willingly signs and executes this instrument as the Will of the Testator, that each of us in the presence and hearing of the Testator and the other Witness who is signing hereby signs this Will to act as witnesses to the Testator's signing, and to the best of our knowledge the Testator is 18 years of age or older, of sound mind, and under no constraint or undue influence.

_____   _____
Signature of Witness #1   Address of Witness #1

_____   _____
Signature of Witness #2   Address of Witness #2

CHAPTER 9
FORM 3: SELF-PROVING AFFIDAVIT

FORM CAN BE DONE TO HELP WITH THE WORK OF USING A WILL LATER

This form is optional but can be done with a Will to help with the legal work involved in later using a Will after a death. This form is a statutory form that is found in law at Kentucky Revised Statutes § 394.225.

FORM HELPS SHOW A WILL WAS PROPERLY SIGNED

The Self-Proving Affidavit helps "prove" a Will was signed properly. If this form isn't done then after a death a little more work is needed to get evidence from either witnesses to the Will signing, persons familiar with signatures of people, or a handwriting expert. Without the Self-Proving Affidavit there is a bit more legal risk a Will won't be followed later. But of people doing Wills about half skip a Self-Proving Affidavit mostly due to the hassle of finding a notary on top of 2 witnesses each time a Will is done, and since it requires extra work by the person doing a Will mostly just to save later work of people happy to be getting things under a Will.

FORM IS DONE BY TESTATOR AND 2 WITNESSES SIGNING WITH A NOTARY

For this form to be valid a person who is a notary (also called a "notary public") must see the Testator and 2 witnesses sign this form and then the notary notarizes the form. A notary can be found and asked to help at a bank, copy-mail center, brokers, insurance agents, library, court, government office, and many other places (using a phonebook to find a helpful notary is common). This form is often signed a few minutes after a Will is signed but it can be done later (even years later) when all can meet with a notary. But this Affidavit form can't legally be done before the Will it supports is done. This form when completed is often kept paper-clipped to the Will it supports.

SELF-PROVING AFFIDAVIT

STATE OF KENTUCKY

COUNTY OF _____

      Before me, the undersigned authority, on this day personally appeared _____ and _____ known to me to be the Testator and the Witnesses, respectively, whose names are signed to the attached or foregoing instrument and, all of these persons being by me first duly sworn. _____, the Testator, declared to me and to the Witnesses in my presence that the instrument is the Will of the Testator and the Testator had willingly signed or directed another to sign for the Testator, and that the Testator executed it as Testator's free and voluntary act for the purposes therein expressed; and each of the Witnesses stated to me, in the presence and hearing of the Testator, that each Witness signed the Will to act as witness in the presence of the Testator and of the other subscribing Witness, and that to the best of the knowledge of each Witness the Testator was 18 years of age or over, of sound mind and under no constraint or undue influence.

                                  _____
                                  Testator

_____   _____
Witness   Witness

Subscribed, sworn and acknowledged before me by _____, the Testator, subscribed and sworn before me by _____ and _____, the Witnesses, this _____ day of _____, 20___.

_____
Signature
Official Capacity Of Officer:_____

CHAPTER 10
FORM 4: HANDWRITTEN WILL

WILL CAN SKIP USING THE NORMAL 2 WITNESSES IF IT'S HANDWRITTEN
A Handwritten Will is a Will that is easier to do since it doesn't need 2 witnesses if it is all handwritten.

HANDWRITTEN WILL WITHOUT WITNESSES IS ALLOWED IN MAINE
In 27 states including Kentucky a person doing a Will can skip the usual legal need for 2 witnesses if : 1) it is all handwritten by the person doing the Will (not photocopied, typed, computer printed, or handwritten by anyone else), and 2) it is signed and dated. Many people call this a "Handwritten Will" and many lawyers call this a "Holographic Will" for various reasons. Handwritten Wills are allowed since handwriting is hard to fake, people may be in an emergency or rush, witnesses may be scarce in the countryside, it is private, it can be cheap by skipping complexity and people, and it is traditional to allow this especially in rural places. The 27 states with Handwritten Wills have 55% of the U.S. population. See states with Handwritten Wills on map below in dark.

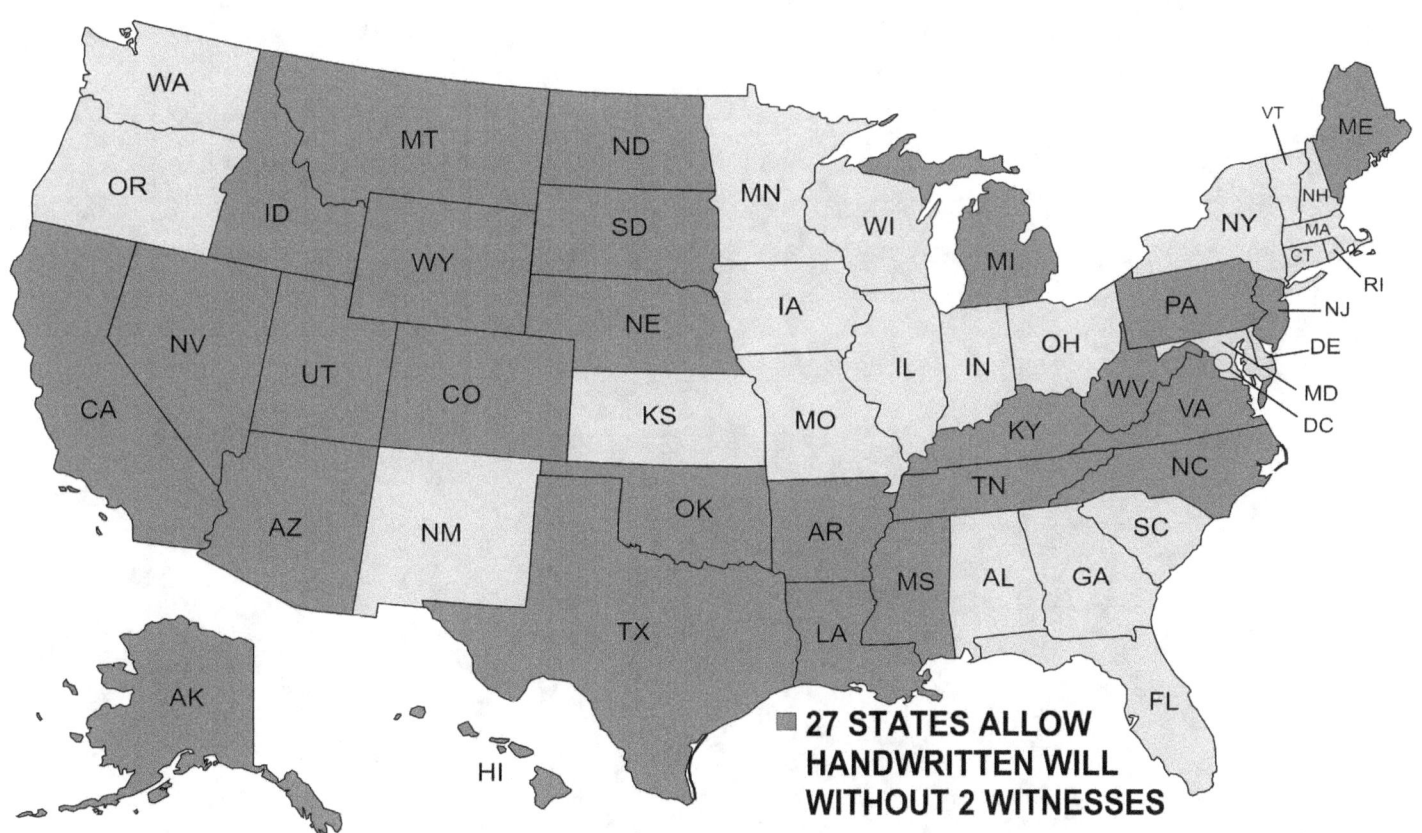

HANDWRITTEN WILLS ARE USUALLY FINE BUT REQUIRE LATER WORK
Some lawyers warn against Handwritten Wills saying they often read confusingly, skip legal words that help in some cases, and are found invalid more often – but some studies show they are liked and usually fine. To use a Handwritten Will later after a death some people must in writing or in testimony say the handwriting looks like the Testator's, which can be a hassle. But a normal Will if no Self-Proving Affidavit was done also needs similar proof like from a witness to the signing or other proof of signing. Handwritten Wills tend to be done by people who are young so unlikely to need a Will soon, who are in a hurry, who want to fix a mistake, who before a trip want to pick a Guardian, who moved to a new state, or who plan to do a better Will later.

WORDS BELOW ON THIS PAGE CAN BE USED FOR A HANDWRITTEN WILL

People can do a Handwritten Will in a sentence that is legal but may leave out helpful parts, for example: *"As my Will I give my estate and all else to Ann Baker who shall be Executor. – Dan Baker"* But it is recommended people use more complex words for a Handwritten Will shown on this page below. To do this people should change the names and words below on this page to match what they want done. If some people named to get things later die it is best to quickly re-do the Will and name different people. The last paragraph about Guardians for children can be skipped if a person has no children under age 18. This Will must be all handwritten by the person doing it on some paper (pencil is allowed) and then signed and dated by the person (usually in pen or permanent marker).

WILL

1. I am John Max Hill and I now live in Jefferson County, Kentucky. I revoke any prior Wills and Codicils and declare this to be my Will.

2. I give my estate and all else to Jane Eve Hill and Wendy Sue Baker. My not giving to some other family of mine is intentional.

3. I name Jane Eve Hill as Personal Representative for me, my Will, and my estate. I request informal probate.

4. No bond, surety, or similar is needed for any Personal Representative, Guardian of any type, or other fiduciary.

5. If ever needed for a minor child of mine I name Mary Ann Dodd my sister as Guardian to have care, custody, and control of them. I name this same person to be Guardian with control and power over any minor child's property, money, and estate.

May 8, 2024   *John Max Hill*

CHAPTER 11
FORM 5: LIVING WILL DIRECTIVE AND HEALTH CARE SURROGATE DESIGNATION

FORM CAN GIVE INSTRUCTIONS, PICK PERSON, AND COVER STOPPING CARE

This form lets a person give health care instructions and name a person to control health care if needed. This long form is not usually followed by paramedics and others who are in a hurry outside of some facility. This book's form is the well known form written by the Kentucky Attorney General that is found online at *https://www.ag.ky.gov*.

IN FIRST PART A PERSON CAN BE NAMED AS SURROGATE TO CONTROL CARE

The form's first part lets a person name someone to be "Health Care Surrogate" to have power to make medical decisions if the person is later incapacitated (if they can't communicate, be rational, or be awake enough to control care by themselves). Some people call this part the "Health Care Power Of Attorney" part. Often named as Surrogate is a spouse, adult child, relative, or friend. Naming a family member as Surrogate can avoid their need to rush to see a judge to get more power later. Anyone associated with a place giving care usually should not be named as Surrogate, including doctors or nurses. The form has a spot to put a 2nd person to serve if the first person doesn't serve, but most people skip this since it's rarely needed. A Surrogate can use some judgment but must follow written instructions and also should do what a person would want done. Many people use the form to name a Surrogate and then skip the rest.

IN LATER PART ("LIVING WILL" PART) CAN SAY DOCTORS CAN STOP CARE

The form's later part is the "Living Will Directive", and this lets a person say whether care should stop if later doctors think an incapacitated person is in very bad health and more health care likely won't help. The form has a few options on this. But instead of doing this many people think a Surrogate should control stopping care so they skip most parts and just do the "*Surrogate Determination of Best Interest*" question to say the Surrogate can decide when to stop care. A doctor often helps explain the form to their patient.

PERSON SIGNS FORM IN FRONT OF NOTARY OR 2 WITNESSES

To complete the form a person signs with 2 witnesses at least age 18 who then sign or, alternatively, in front of a person who is a notary who then notarizes the form. A person need not do both. A witness can't be named Surrogate in the form, can't be involved with giving care so not any employee at place giving care, can't be likely to benefit from person's death, and can't be financially responsible for the person's health care (so not a spouse or parent of minor child). Usually the form is quickly shown to any place that might give care to copy in a person's file to follow. A person can keep the completed form till needed or immediately can hand it to a Surrogate or family members to have to use. To cancel the form a person can tell any Surrogate and any doctor or places shown the form that it is canceled.

KENTUCKY LIVING WILL DIRECTIVE AND HEALTH CARE SURROGATE DESIGNATION OF

_____
(PRINTED NAME)

_____
(DATE OF BIRTH)

My wishes regarding life-prolonging treatment and artificially provided nutrition and hydration to be provided to me if I no longer have decisional capacity, have a terminal condition, or become permanently unconscious have been indicated by checking and initialing the appropriate lines below.

HEALTH CARE SURROGATE DESIGNATION

By checking and initialing the line below, I specifically:

☐ _____ (check box and initial line, if you desire to name a surrogate)

Designate _____ as my health care surrogate(s) to make health care decisions for me in accordance with this directive when I no longer have decisional capacity. If _____ refuses or is not able to act for me, I designate _____ as my health care surrogate(s). Any prior designation is revoked.

LIVING WILL DIRECTIVE

If I do not designate a surrogate, the following are my directions to my attending physician. If I have designated a surrogate, my surrogate shall comply with my wishes as indicated below. By checking and initialing the lines below, I specifically:

Life Prolonging Treatment (check and initial only one)

☐ _____ (check box and initial line, if you desire the option below)
Direct that treatment be withheld or withdrawn, and that I be permitted to die naturally with only the administration of medication or the performance of any medical treatment deemed necessary to alleviate pain.

☐ _____ (check box and initial line, if you desire the option below)
DO NOT authorize that life-prolonging treatment be withheld or withdrawn.

Nourishment and/or Fluids (check and initial only one)

☐ _____ (check box and initial line, if you desire the option below)
Authorize the withholding or withdrawal of artificially provided food, water, or other artificially provided nourishment or fluids.

LIVING WILL DIRECTIVE — CONTINUED

☐ _____ (check box and initial line, if you desire the option below)
DO NOT authorize the withholding or withdrawal of artificially provided food, water, or other artificially provided nourishment or fluids.

Surrogate Determination of Best Interest

NOTE: If you desire this option, DO NOT choose any of the preceding options regarding Life Prolonging Treatment and Nourishment and/ or Fluids

☐ _____ (check box and initial line, if you desire the option below)
Authorize my surrogate, as designated on the previous page, to withhold or withdraw artificially provided nourishment or fluids, or other treatment if the surrogate determines that withholding or withdrawing is in my best interest; but I do not mandate that withholding or withdrawing.

Organ/Tissue/Eye Donation

I certify that I am eighteen (18) years of age or older and of sound mind, and that upon my death, I hereby give:

Check appropriate boxes and initial the line beside that box:

☐ _____ Any needed organs, tissues, and eye/corneas

OR

The following organs or tissues only (check and initial all that apply):

☐ _____ All needed organs
☐ _____ All needed tissues
☐ _____ Corneas
☐ _____ Eyes
☐ _____ Other

OR

☐ _____ Only the specified organs/tissues as listed:

_____

_____

_____

Organs that can be donated: heart, lungs, liver, pancreas, kidneys, and small bowel.

Tissues that can currently be donated: skin (outermost layer from lower trunk and abdomen), bone, heart valves, leg veins, pericardium, vertebral bodies.

Eye donation can be the corneas (outer most layer), the sclera (shell), or the entire eye.

In the absence of my ability to give directions regarding the use of life-prolonging treatment and artificially provided nutrition and hydration, it is my intention that this directive shall be honored by my attending physician, my family, and any surrogate designated pursuant to this directive as the final expression of my legal right to refuse medical or surgical treatment and I accept the consequences of the refusal.

If I have been diagnosed as pregnant and that diagnosis is known to my attending physician, this directive shall have no force or effect during the course of my pregnancy.

I understand the full import of this directive and I am emotionally and mentally competent to make this directive.

Signed this _____ day of _____, 20_____

_____
(signature and address of the grantor)

Have two adults witness your signature OR have signature notarized.*

In our joint presence, the grantor, who is of sound mind and eighteen (18) years of age, or older, voluntarily dated and signed this writing or directed it to be dated and signed for the grantor.

_____
(signature and address of witness)

_____
(signature and address of witness)

OR

COMMONWEALTH OF KENTUCKY, _____ County

Before me, the undersigned authority, came the grantor who is of sound mind and eighteen (18) years of age or older, and acknowledged that he/she voluntarily dated and signed this writing or directed it to be signed and dated as above.

Done this _____ day of _____, 20_____

_____   _____
Signature of Notary Public   Date commission expires

* *None of the following shall be a witness to or serve as a notary public or other person authorized to administer oaths in regard to any advance directive made under this section:*
    a) *A blood relative of the grantor;*
    b) *A beneficiary of the grantor under descent and distribution statutes of the Commonwealth;*
    c) *An employee of a health care facility in which the grantor is a patient, unless the employee serves as a notary public;*
    d) *An attending physician of the grantor; or*
    e) *Any person directly financially responsible for the grantor's health care.*

NOTICE: *Execution of this document restricts withholding and withdrawing of some medical procedures. Consult Kentucky Revised Statutes or your attorney.*

A person designated as a surrogate pursuant to an advance directive may resign at any time by giving written notice to the grantor; to the immediate successor surrogate, if any; to the attending physician; and to any health care facility which is then waiting for the surrogate to make a health care decision.

CHAPTER 12
FORM 6: DO NOT RESUSCITATE

IN FORM CAN IMMEDIATELY REFUSE MOST HEALTH CARE

This chapter actually has 2 forms that are similar and do the very serious act of saying to immediately no longer give most or certain health care. Doing this is rare and usually only the sickest or oldest people do it. Both forms are often called the "Do Not Resuscitate" or "DNR" form, and people very rarely do both forms. Both forms are short and usually will be followed by paramedics and other people outside of a health facility. The forms are found many places like the Office Of Emergency Medical Services at oems.nc.gov/dnr-most.

FIRST FORM SAYS TO IMMEDIATELY NOT GIVE MANY KINDS OF CARE

This chapter's first form, the "Medical Orders For Scope Of Treatment" form (the "M.O.S.T." form), says to immediately not give the many kinds of health care selected in it. This form can say to immediately no longer try C.P.R., antibiotics, and artificial feeding. This form is short so it can be read quickly and followed by those in a hurry like paramedics outside any care facility, but this form also can be used by people who are in a care facility. Pain relief and comfort care is usually still given, so paramedics are still usually called if needed to get this. After doing this form a person is usually free to override it by clearly requesting care from a doctor, paramedic, or other person. In recent years the M.O.S.T. form is more often used to say to immediately not give most care, and other forms are less often used including this chapter's second form.

SECOND FORM SAYS TO IMMEDIATELY NOT TRY RESUSCITATION

This chapter's second form, the "Do Not Resuscitate Order" form (also called the "D-N-R" form), says to immediately not give any "resuscitation". Resuscitation is trying to restart or help with breathing or the heart and usually covers cardio-pulmonary resuscitation (C.P.R.), defibrillation (electric shocks), and machine or tube breathing. This form is short so it can be read quickly and followed by those in a hurry like paramedics and other people outside any care facility, but this form also can be used by people who are in a care facility. Pain relief and comfort care is usually still given, so paramedics are still usually called if needed to get this. After doing this form a person is usually free to override it by requesting care from a doctor or other person.

FORM IS SIGNED BY DOCTOR OR SIMILAR AND THEN THE PATIENT

To be valid these forms must be signed by a person's doctor (physician) or some other similar health professional, and usually by the person doing it (or their named representative if authorized to do this). Once done a person usually shows the form to places that may give care to add to medical files to follow. Often people also keep a copy near their body to show to paramedics or others who may try to give care. Some people who do this form get a bracelet that shows the form has been done which a doctor can get. The M.O.S.T. form often is on paper with bits of red and the Do Not Resuscitate Order form often is on solid yellow paper.

HIPAA PERMITS DISCLOSURE OF MOST TO OTHER HEALTH CARE PROFESSIONALS AS NECESSARY			
MOST Medical Orders for Scope of Treatment This document is based on this person's medical condition and wishes. Any section not completed indicates a preference for full treatment for that section.		Patient's Last Name:	Effective Date of Form: _____ Form must be reviewed at least annually.
		Patient's First Name, Middle Initial:	Patient's Date of Birth:

Section A
Check One Box Only

CARDIOPULMONARY RESUSCITATION (CPR): PERSON HAS NO PULSE AND IS NOT BREATHING.
- ❑ Attempt Resuscitation (CPR)
- ❑ Do Not Attempt Resuscitation

When not in cardiopulmonary arrest, follow orders in **B**, **C**, and **D**.

Section B
Check One Box Only

MEDICAL INTERVENTIONS: PERSON HAS PULSE OR IS BREATHING.
- ❑ **Full Scope of Treatment:** Use intubation, advanced airway interventions, mechanical ventilation, defibrillation or cardioversion as indicated, medical treatment, IV fluids, and provide comfort measures. **Transfer to a hospital if indicated. Includes intensive care. Treatment Plan: Full treatment including life support measures.**
- ❑ **Limited Additional Intervention:** Use medical treatment, oral and IV medications, IV fluids, cardiac monitoring as indicated, non-invasive bi-level positive airway pressure, a bag valve mask, and comfort measures. Do not use intubation or mechanical ventilation. **Transfer to hospital if indicated. Avoid intensive care. Treatment Plan: Provide basic medical treatments.**
- ❑ **Comfort Measures:** Keep clean, warm and dry. Use medication by any route. Positioning, wound care and other measures to relieve pain and suffering. Use oxygen, suction and manual treatment of airway obstruction as needed for comfort. **Do not transfer to hospital** unless comfort needs cannot be met in the patient's current location (e.g. hip fracture).

Other Instructions _____

Section C
Check One Box Only

ANTIBIOTICS
- ❑ Antibiotics if indicated for the purpose of maintaining life
- ❑ Determine use or limitation of antibiotics when infection occurs.
- ❑ Use of antibiotics to relieve pain and discomfort.
- ❑ No Antibiotics (use other measures to relieve symptoms).

Other instructions: _____

Section D
Check One Box Only in Each Column

MEDICALLY ADMINISTERED FLUIDS AND NUTRITION: the provision of nutrition and fluids, even if medically administered, is a basic human right and authorization to deny or withdraw shall be limited to the patient, the surrogate in accordance with KRS 311.629, or the responsible party in accordance with KRS 311.631.

- ❑ **Long term IV fluids if indicated**
- ❑ **IV fluids for a defined trial period.** Goal:_____
- ❑ **No IV fluids** (provide other measures to ensure comfort)

- ❑ **Long term feeding tube if indicated**
- ❑ **Feeding tube for a defined trial period.** Goal:_____
- ❑ **No feeding tube**

Special instructions _____

Section E
Check The Appropriate Box

Directions were given:
- ❑ Orally
- ❑ Written

Patient Preferences as a Basis for This MOST Form:
Basis for order must be documented in medical record.

- ❑ Adult Patient with decisional capacity
- ❑ Parent/guardian of minor patient
- ❑ Surrogate per advance directive
- ❑ Judicially appointed guardian/durable power of attorney with power to make health care decisions
- ❑ Spouse
- ❑ Majority of patient's reasonably available adult children
- ❑ Parent
- ❑ Majority of patient's reasonably available nearest living relatives of same relation

- ❑ Patient does not have an advance medical directive such as a living will or health care power of attorney.
- ❑ Patient has an advance medical directive such as a living will or health care power of attorney in place. I certify this form is in accordance with the decisions in the current advance medical directive.

Name: Printed: _____ Position: _____ Signature: _____

I agree that adequate information has been provided and significant thought has been given to decisions outlined in this form. Treatment preferences have been expressed to the physician (MD/DO). This document reflects those treatment preferences and indicates informed consent. *If signed by a patient, surrogate or responsible party, preferences expressed must reflect patient's wishes as best understood by that surrogate or responsible party.* **You are not required to sign this form to receive treatment.**

Patient, Surrogate or Responsible Party:	Signature:	Relationship: Contact #:	
Health Care Professional Preparing Form: Print Name	Health Care Professional Preparing Form: Signature	Preferred Phone #:	Date Prepared:
Physician Signature	Physician (Print Name)	Physician Contact Number	

SEND FORM WITH PATIENT/RESIDENT WHEN TRANSFERRED OR DISCHARGED

INFORMATION FOR PATIENT, SURROGATE OR RESPONSIBLE PARTY OF PATIENT NAMED ON THIS FORM
- The MOST form is always voluntary and is usually for persons with advanced illness. MOST records your wishes for medical treatment in your current state of health. The provision of nutrition and fluids, even if medically administered, is a basic human right and authorization to deny or withdraw shall be limited to the patient, the surrogate in accordance with KRS 311.629, or the responsible party in accordance with KRS 311.631. Once initial medical treatment is begun and the risks and benefits of further therapy are clear, your treatment wishes may change. Your medical care and this form can be changed to reflect your new wishes at any time. However, no form can address all the medical treatment decisions that may need to be made. An advance directive, such as the Kentucky Health Care Power of Attorney, is recommended for all capable adults, regardless of their health status. An advance directive allows you to document in detail your future health care instructions or name a surrogate to speak for you if you are unable to speak for yourself, or both. If there are conflicting directions between an enforceable living will and a MOST form, the provisions of the living will shall prevail.

DIRECTIONS FOR COMPLETING AND IMPLEMENTING FORM

COMPLETING MOST
- MOST must be reviewed, prepared and signed by the patient's physician in personal communication with the patient, the patient's surrogate or responsible party.
- MOST must be reviewed and contain the original signature of the patient's physician to be valid. **Be sure to document the basis in the progress notes of the medical record**. Mode of communication (e.g., in person, by telephone, etc.) should also be documented.
- The signature of the patient, surrogate or a responsible party is required; however, if the patient's surrogate or a responsible party is not reasonably available to sign the original form, a copy of the completed form with the signature of the patient's surrogate or a responsible party must be signed by the patient's physician and placed in the medical record.
- Use of original form is required. **Be sure to send the original form with the patient**.
- **There is no requirement that a patient have a MOST.**

IMPLEMENTING MOST
- If a health care provider or facility cannot comply with the orders due to policy or personal ethics, the provider or facility must arrange for transfer of the patient to another provider or facility.

REVIEWING MOST
This MOST must be reviewed at least annually or earlier if:
- The patient is admitted and/or discharged from a health care facility;
- There is a substantial change in the patient's health status; or
- The patient's treatment preferences change.
- If MOST is revised or becomes invalid, draw a line through sections A – E and write "VOID" in large letters.

REVOCATION OF MOST
This MOST may be revoked by the patient, the surrogate or the responsible party.

Review of MOST				
Review Date	Reviewer and Location of Review	MD/DO Signature (Required)	Signature of Patient, Surrogate or Responsible Party (Required)	Outcome of Review, describing the outcome in each row by selecting one of the following:
				❏ No Change ❏ FORM VOIDED, new form completed ❏ FORM VOIDED, **no** new form
				❏ No Change ❏ FORM VOIDED, new form completed ❏ FORM VOIDED, **no** new form

SEND FORM WITH PATIENT/RESIDENT WHEN TRANSFERRED OR DISCHARGED

PAGE INTENTIONALLY LEFT BLANK

Kentucky Emergency Medical Services
Do Not Resuscitate (DNR) Order

Person's Full Legal Name _____

Surrogate's Full Legal Name (if applicable) _____

I, the undersigned person or surrogate who has been designated to make health care decisions in accordance with Kentucky Revised Statutes, hereby direct that in the event of my cardiac or respiratory arrest that this **DO NOT RESUSCITATE (DNR) ORDER** be honored. I understand that DNR means that if my heart stops beating or if I stop breathing, no medical procedure to restart breathing or heart function, more specifically the insertion of a tube into the lungs, or electrical shocking of the heart or cardiopulmonary resuscitation (CPR) will be started by emergency medical services (EMS) personnel.

I understand this decision will *not* prevent emergency medical services personnel from providing other medical care.

I understand that I may revoke this DNR order at any time by destroying this form, removing the DNR bracelet, or by telling the EMS personnel that I want to be resuscitated. Any attempt to alter or change the content, names, or signatures on the EMS DNR form shall make the DNR form invalid.

I understand that this form, or a standard EMS DNR bracelet must be available and must be shown to EMS personnel as soon as they arrive. If the form or bracelet is not provided, the EMS personnel will follow their normal protocols which could include cardiopulmonary resuscitation (CPR) or other resuscitation procedures. I understand that should I die, EMS personnel will require this form and/or bracelet for their records.

I give permission for information about this EMS DNR Order to be given to the prehospital emergency medical care personnel, physicians, nurses, or other health care personnel as necessary to implement this directive.

I hereby state that this *'Do Not Resuscitate (DNR) Order'* is my authentic wish not be resuscitated.

_____   _____
Person/Legal Surrogate Signature   Date

Commonwealth of Kentucky   County of _____

Subscribed and sworn to before me by _____ to be his/her own free act and deed, this _____ day of _____, 20_____.

_____, Notary Public
My commission expires: _____

In lieu of having this Form notarized, it may be witnessed by two persons not related to the individual noted above.

WITNESSED BY:

1. _____

2. _____

This EMS Do Not Resuscitate Form was approved by the Kentucky Board of Medical Licensure at their March 1995 meeting.

Complete the portion below, cut out, fold, and insert in DNR bracelet
I certify that an EMS Do Not Resuscitate (DNR) form has been executed.
Person's Name (print or type) _____
Person's or Legal Surrogate's Signature _____

KENTUCKY EMERGENCY MEDICAL SERVICES
DO NOT RESUSCITATE (DNR) ORDER

INSTRUCTIONS

PURPOSE

This standardized EMS DNR Order has been developed and approved by the Kentucky Board of Medical Licensure, in consultation with the Cabinet for Human Resources. It is in compliance with KRS Chapter 311 as amended by Senate Bill 311 passed by the 1994 General Assembly, which directs the Kentucky Board of Medical Licensure to develop a standard form to authorize EMS providers to honor advance directives to withhold or terminate care.

For covered persons in cardiac or respiratory arrest, resuscitative measures to be withheld include external chest compressions, intubation, defibrillation, administration of cardiac medications and artificial respiration. The EMS DNR Order does **not** affect the provision of other emergency medical care, including oxygen administration, suctioning, control of bleeding, administration of analgesics and comfort care.

APPLICABILITY

This **EMS DNR Order** applies only to resuscitation attempts by health care providers in the **prehospital** setting(i.e., certified EMT-First Responders, Emergency Medical Technicians, and Paramedics) — in patients' homes, in a long-term care facility, during transport to or from a health care facility, or in other locations outside acute care hospitals.

INSTRUCTIONS

Any adult person may execute an EMS DNR Order. The person for whom the Order is executed shall sign and date the Order and my either have the Order notarized by a Kentucky Notary Public or have their signature witness by two persons not related to them. The executor of the Order must also place their printed or typed name in the designated area and their signature on the EMS DNR Order bracelet insert found at the bottom of the EMS DNR Order form. The bracelet insert shall be detached and placed in a hospital type bracelet and placed on the wrist or ankle of the executor of the Order.

If the person for whom the EMS DNR Order is contemplated is unable to give informed consent, or is a minor, the person's legal surrogate shall sign and date the Order and may either have the form notarized by a Kentucky Notary Public or have their signature witnessed by two persons not related to the person for which the form is being executed or related to the legal health care surrogate. The legal health care surrogate shall also complete the required information on the EMS DNR bracelet insert found at the bottom of the EMS DNR Order form. The bracelet shall be detached and placed in a hospital type bracelet and placed on the wrist or ankle of the person for which this Order was executed.

The original, completed EMS DNR Order or the EMS DNR Bracelet must be readily available to EMS personnel in order for the EMS DNR Order to be honored. Resuscitation attempts may be initiated until the form or bracelet is presented and the identity of the patient is confirmed by the EMS personnel. It is recommended that the EMS DNR Order be displayed in a prominent place close to the patient and/or the bracelet be on the patient's wrist or ankle.

REVOCATION

An EMS DNR Order may be revoked at any time orally or by performing an act such as burning, tearing, canceling, obliterating or by destroying the order by the person on whose behalf it was executed or by the person's legal health care surrogate.

IT SHOULD BE UNDERSTOOD BY THE PERSON EXECUTING THIS EMS DNR ORDER OR THEIR LEGAL HEALTH CARE SURROGATE, THAT SHOULD THE PERSON LISTED ON THE EMS DNR ORDER DIE WHILE EMS PREHOSPITAL PERSONNEL ARE IN ATTENDANCE, THE EMS DNR ORDER OR EMS DNR BRACELET MUST BE GIVEN TO THE EMS PREHOSPITAL PERSONNEL FOR THEIR RECORDS.

CHAPTER 13
FORM 7: STATUTORY FORM POWER OF ATTORNEY

FORM LETS PERSON SHARE POWER OVER THEIR PROPERTY AND MONEY

This form lets a person share power with someone to let them do things with the person's money, property, debt, and more. Some people call this a "Financial Power of Attorney". This form is a statutory form found in state law at Kentucky Revised Statutes § 457.420.

FORM GIVES POWER TO LET SOMEONE DO THINGS

This form lets a person share power to do things with their money, property, records, and other things with someone trusted like a spouse, other family member, or a friend. The person giving power is usually called the "Principal", and the person getting power is usually called the "Agent" (or the "Attorney in Fact"). If a person is sick or busy this form can let someone else pay bills, use accounts, buy or sell items, borrow, hire workers, sign contracts, see records, and more. This form can avoid more serious legal options like a guardianship or conservatorship done at a court. <u>A person who isn't incapacitated can usually overrule or fire their Agent anytime</u>. Importantly this form is "durable" which means it still is effective if the person who did the form is later incapacitated, but all power of the form ends at the person's death.

IN FORM POWERS GIVEN ARE INITIALED AND INSTRUCTIONS CAN BE GIVEN

A person <u>must initial lines in the form to say which powers are given</u>. Many people in the early part, the <u>Grant Of General Authority</u> section, <u>do</u> give all these powers since if an Agent's power is not clear a bank, school, or other parties may hesitate or refuse to obey the Agent's orders. But most people in the later part, the <u>Grant Of Specific Authority section</u>, <u>do not</u> give these powers since these powers are less often needed and are riskier to give. <u>In the form a person can say who'd they want as Guardian or Conservator</u> if a judge ever finds it needed, but many people don't bother with this.

DUE TO RISKS MANY SKIP THIS FORM OR CONSULT A LAWYER

Many people skip this form or first see a lawyer. Using this form is risky and can lead to harm since the Agent can be wasteful with money, commit fraud or theft, or by carelessness allow some other harms. A person acting as Agent has a duty to be loyal and act reasonably and can be sued for any harm, but they may later be out of money to pay. Usually banks and others can't be blamed for obeying an Agent's orders. The law is complex and basic acts of an Agent may be fine like paying bills but some acts may be improper like making gifts, risky investments, or unusual acts. It is best a person not the Agent do anything unusual.

PEOPLE SHOULD SIGN USUALLY WITH A NOTARY

The form is usually signed by a person in front of someone who is a notary who then notarizes the form. The signed form can be kept by a person until needed or can be quickly given to the named Agent to hold and use when needed. To cancel the form the person should tell the Agent and take back copies and also maybe tell all places that saw the form that it is canceled. The last page is an "Agent Certification" page which later some banks may ask the Agent to sign.

KENTUCKY
STATUTORY FORM POWER OF ATTORNEY

IMPORTANT INFORMATION

This power of attorney authorizes another person (your agent) to make decisions concerning your property for you (the principal). Your agent will be able to make decisions and act with respect to your property (including your money) whether or not you are able to act for yourself. The meaning of authority over subjects listed on this form is explained in the Uniform Power of Attorney Act in KRS Chapter 457.

This power of attorney does not authorize the agent to make health-care decisions for you.

You should select someone you trust to serve as your agent. Unless you specify otherwise, generally the agent's authority will continue until you die or revoke the power of attorney or the agent resigns or is unable to act for you.

Your agent is entitled to reasonable compensation unless you state otherwise in the Special Instructions.

This form provides for designation of one (1) agent. If you wish to name more than one (1) agent you may name a coagent in the Special Instructions. Coagents are not required to act together unless you include that requirement in the Special Instructions.

If your agent is unable or unwilling to act for you, your power of attorney will end unless you have named a successor agent. You may also name a second successor agent.

This power of attorney becomes effective immediately unless you state otherwise in the Special Instructions.

If you have questions about the power of attorney or the authority you are granting to your agent, you should seek legal advice before signing this form.

DESIGNATION OF AGENT

I, _____, name the following person as my agent:
(Name of Principal)

Name of Agent: _____
Agent's Address: _____
Agent's Telephone Number: _____

DESIGNATION OF SUCCESSOR AGENT(S) (OPTIONAL)

If my agent is unable or unwilling to act for me, I name as my successor agent:

Name of Successor Agent: _____
Successor Agent's Address: _____
Successor Agent's Telephone Number: _____

GRANT OF GENERAL AUTHORITY

I grant my agent and any successor agent general authority to act for me with respect to the following subjects as defined in the Uniform Power of Attorney Act in KRS Chapter 457:

(INITIAL each subject you want to include in the agent's general authority. If you wish to grant general authority over all of the subjects you may initial "All Preceding Subjects" instead of initialing each subject.)

(_____) Real Property
(_____) Tangible Personal Property
(_____) Stocks and Bonds
(_____) Commodities and Options
(_____) Banks and Other Financial Institutions
(_____) Operation of Entity or Business
(_____) Insurance and Annuities
(_____) Estates, Trusts, and Other Beneficial Interests
(_____) Claims and Litigation
(_____) Personal and Family Maintenance
(_____) Benefits from Governmental Programs or Civil or Military Service
(_____) Retirement Plans
(_____) Taxes
(_____) All Preceding Subjects

GRANT OF SPECIFIC AUTHORITY (OPTIONAL)

My agent MAY NOT do any of the following specific acts for me UNLESS I have INITIALED the specific authority listed below:

(CAUTION: Granting any of the following will give your agent the authority to take actions that could significantly reduce your property or change how your property is distributed at your death. INITIAL ONLY the specific authority you WANT to give your agent.)

(_____) Create, amend, revoke, or terminate an inter vivos trust
(_____) Make a gift, subject to the limitations of the Uniform Power of Attorney Act in KRS 457.400 and any special instructions in this power of attorney
(_____) Create or change rights of survivorship
(_____) Create or change a beneficiary designation
(_____) Authorize another person to exercise authority granted under this power of attorney
(_____) Waive the principal's right to be a beneficiary of a joint and survivor annuity, including a survivor benefit under a retirement plan
(_____) Exercise fiduciary powers that the principal has authority to delegate
(_____) Access the content of electronic communications

LIMITATION ON AGENT'S AUTHORITY

An agent that is not my ancestor, spouse, or descendant MAY NOT use my property to benefit the agent or a person to whom the agent owes an obligation of support unless I have included that authority in the Special Instructions.

SPECIAL INSTRUCTIONS (OPTIONAL)

You may give special instructions on the following lines:

_____
_____
_____
_____
_____
_____
_____
_____
_____
_____
_____
_____
_____
_____
_____
_____
_____
_____
_____
_____
_____

EFFECTIVE DATE

This power of attorney is effective immediately unless I have stated otherwise in the Special Instructions.

NOMINATION OF CONSERVATOR OR GUARDIAN (OPTIONAL)

If it becomes necessary for a court to appoint a conservator of my estate or guardian of my person, I nominate the following person(s) for appointment:

Name of Nominee for conservator of my estate: _____

Nominee's Address: _____

Nominee's Telephone Number: _____

Name of Nominee for guardian of my person: _____

Nominee's Address: _____

Nominee's Telephone Number: _____

RELIANCE ON THIS POWER OF ATTORNEY

Any person, including my agent, may rely upon the validity of this power of attorney or a copy of it unless that person knows it has terminated or is invalid.

SIGNATURE AND ACKNOWLEDGMENT

_____   _____
Your Signature   Date

_____   _____
Your Name Printed   Your Telephone Number

_____
Your Address

STATE OF KENTUCKY

COUNTY OF _____

This document was acknowledged before me on _____ (Date) by_____.
      (Name of Principal)

_____   (Seal, if any)
Signature of Notary
My commission expires: _____

This document prepared by: _____

IMPORTANT INFORMATION FOR AGENT

Agent's Duties

When you accept the authority granted under this power of attorney, a special legal relationship is created between you and the principal. This relationship imposes upon you legal duties that continue until you resign or the power of attorney is terminated or revoked.

You must:
(1) Do what you know the principal reasonably expects you to do with the principal's property or, if you do not know the principal's expectations, act in the principal's best interest;
(2) Act in good faith;
(3) Do nothing beyond the authority granted in this power of attorney; and
(4) Disclose your identity as an agent whenever you act for the principal by writing or printing the name of the principal and signing your own name as "agent" in the following manner: **(Principal's Name) by (Your Signature) as Agent**

Unless the Special Instructions in this power of attorney state otherwise, you must also:
(1) Act loyally for the principal's benefit;
(2) Avoid conflicts that would impair your ability to act in the principal's best interest;
(3) Act with care, competence, and diligence;
(4) Keep a record of all receipts, disbursements, and transactions made on behalf of the principal;
(5) Cooperate with any person that has authority to make health-care decisions for the principal to do what you know the principal reasonably expects or, if you do not know the principal's expectations, to act in the principal's best interest; and
(6) Attempt to preserve the principal's estate plan if you know the plan and preserving the plan is consistent with the principal's best interest.

TERMINATION OF AGENT'S AUTHORITY

You must stop acting on behalf of the principal if you learn of any event that terminates this power of attorney or your authority under this power of attorney. Events that terminate a power of attorney or your authority to act under a power of attorney include:
(1) Death of the principal;
(2) The principal's revocation of the power of attorney or your authority;
(3) The occurrence of a termination event stated in the power of attorney;
(4) The purpose of the power of attorney is fully accomplished; or
(5) If you are married to the principal, a legal action is filed with a court to end your marriage, or for your legal separation, unless the Special Instructions in this power of attorney state that such an action will not terminate your authority.

LIABILITY OF AGENT

The meaning of the authority granted to you is defined in the Uniform Power of Attorney Act in KRS Chapter 457. If you violate the Uniform Power of Attorney Act under KRS Chapter 457 or act outside the authority granted, you may be liable for any damages caused by your violation.

[THIS PAGE FOR USE BY AGENT UPON LATER REQUEST TO CONFIRM POWER OF ATTORNEY STILL IS VALID]

AGENT'S CERTIFICATION AS TO THE VALIDITY OF POWER OF ATTORNEY AND AGENT'S AUTHORITY

STATE OF KENTUCKY, COUNTY OF _____)

I, _____ (Name of Agent), say, declare and certify under penalty of perjury that _____(Name of Principal) granted me authority as an agent or successor agent in a power of attorney dated _____.

I further say, declare and certify that to my knowledge:

(1) the Principal is alive and has not revoked the Power of Attorney or my authority to act under the Power of Attorney and the Power of Attorney and my authority to act under the Power of Attorney have not terminated;

(2) if the Power of Attorney was drafted to become effective upon the happening of an event or contingency, the event or contingency has occurred;

(3) if I was named as a successor agent, the prior agent is no longer able or willing to serve; and

(4) _____
_____
_____
(Insert other relevant statements).

ACCEPTANCE. By signing below the Agent says and declares they accept and agree to act as Agent under the power of attorney described above which imposes fiduciary and other legal responsibilities.

SIGNATURE AND ACKNOWLEDGMENT

_____ _____
(Signature of Agent)   (Date)

_____ Agent's Name Printed
_____ Agent's Address
_____
_____ Agent's Telephone Number

Notary or other officer

State of Kentucky, County of _____
This document was acknowledged before me on _____, 20_____, by
_____ (name of principal).
[Notary Seal]:

_____
(Signature of Notarial Officer)
Notary Public for the Commonwealth of Kentucky
My commission expires: _____

CHAPTER 14
FORM 8: STANDARD POWER OF ATTORNEY FOR MEDICAL / SCHOOL DECISION MAKING

FORM LETS PARENT GIVE POWER TO SOMEONE OVER MINOR CHILD

This form lets a parent or legal guardian give certain power to someone over a child under the age of 18. This form is a standard form issued by the Kentucky court system.

FORM CAN DESIGNATE SOMEONE TO HAVE POWER OVER CHILD

In the form a parent or legal guardian can give someone power over a minor child in issues about health care or schooling. The person who is given power is called the "Attorney In Fact" or less often the "Agent". This form is often used if a parent or child is away from the other for work, school, sports, drug treatment, prison or jail, immigration, military, long visit with family or friends, or if a child is in hospital and needs a person nearby with authority. The form is not usually done for brief or minor situations like a babysitter, day care, week with relative, or cases where parent can come quickly if needed. Using this form may avoid need for some action at court. A parent usually can always fire the Attorney in Fact or overrule a decision.

FORM IS SIGNED BY PERSON WITH A NOTARY

The form must be signed by a person in front of someone who is a notary who then notarizes the form. The signed form can be kept by a person until needed or quickly given to the named Attorney In Fact to hold and use when needed. To cancel the form a person should tell the Attorney In Fact and take back copies and also maybe tell all places that saw the form that it is canceled. Some people have both 2 parents sign the form since this slightly increases the chance that schools, doctors, and others will do as the form says.

AOC-796
Rev. 10-17
Page 1 of 1

Commonwealth of Kentucky
Court of Justice   www.courts.ky.gov

KRS 27A.095

STANDARD POWER OF ATTORNEY FOR MEDICAL/SCHOOL DECISION MAKING

KNOW ALL PERSONS BY THESE PRESENTS:

That I, _____, a resident of _____ (city) _____ (county) _____ (state) residing at _____ (street address) do hereby make, constitute, and appoint _____, residing at _____ (full address) my true and lawful attorney in fact for me and in my name, place and stead, in their sole discretion, to transact, handle and dispose of the limited matters set forth herein, specifically:

To consent to medical treatment for _____, minor child, of whom I am the biological parent, legal custodian or legal guardian. Medical treatment means any medical, chiropractic, optometric, or dental examination, diagnostic procedure, and treatment, including but not limited to hospitalization, developmental screening, mental health screening and treatment, preventive care, pharmacy services, immunizations recommended by the federal Centers for Disease Control and Prevention's Advisory Committee on Immunization Practices, well-child care, and blood testing, except that "medical treatment" shall not include HIV/AIDS testing, controlled substance testing, or any other testing for which a separate court order or informed consent is required under other applicable law.

To make school-related decisions for _____, minor child, of whom I am the biological parent, legal custodian or legal guardian. I hereby affirm that the minor child resides with _____ (attorney in fact) at _____ (full address).

This instrument is intended to, and does hereby, grant to my attorney full power and authority to do and perform each and every act and thing whatsoever requisite, necessary and proper to be done, in the exercise of the rights and powers herein granted, as fully, to all intents and purposes, as I might or could do personally present, hereby ratifying and confirming all that my attorney shall do or cause to be done by virtue thereof.

It is fully understood that any school district asked to recognize the authority assigned by this instrument may regularly review and/or audit the residency of the child. Falsification of this document may constitute a criminal offense.

The rights, powers and authority of my attorney shall commence upon execution of this instrument and shall remain in full force and effect until this instrument is terminated by me in writing.

So acknowledged this _____ **day of** _____, 2_____.

_____
Parent/Legal Guardian's Name *(printed)*

_____
Parent/Legal Guardian's Signature

Subscribed and sworn before me on _____, 2_____.

_____, Notary Public. My commission expires: _____.

THIS IS NOT A COURT ORDER.

The execution or possession of this form does not signify that a person has lawful custody or guardianship of the child mentioned herein. The limited purpose of this form is to indicate that the above-named person given power of attorney has the authority to consent to medical treatment and to make school-related decisions for the above-named child. This form is not required to be filed with the circuit court clerk. <u>Falsification of this document may constitute a criminal offense.</u>

CHAPTER 15
FORM 9: FUNERAL PLANNING DECLARATION

LETS PERSON BE NAMED TO CONTROL FUNERAL AND RELATED MATTERS

This form lets a person name someone to control funeral and related matters like burial, cremation, ceremonies, and special dinners. This form is a standard form put out by the Kentucky court system.

IN FORM CAN NAME PERSON TO CONTROL FUNERAL AND RELATED MATTERS

This form lets a person doing the form, called the "Declarant", name someone as "Designee" with power to control funeral and related matters like burial, cremation, ceremonies, tombstone, dinners, and buying goods and services for all this. <u>If this form isn't done then by law control is by closest family</u> (in order this is a spouse, adult child, parents, brothers/sisters, and then other close family). <u>People actually rarely do this form</u> like only if family will be too upset while mourning to think well, be bad with money, or do unwanted things. Payment for things comes from pre-paid funeral accounts, insurance, and decedent's or estate's money and property, and Executor and family legally must help arrange payment.

DO WHAT DECEASED WANTED FOR THEIR BODILY REMAINS AND EVENTS

The form has spot to pick options and write some instructions, but many people skip this and trust the person given power or their family to be wise or do what was discussed. Some people write instructions just to urge low cost. Note, if after a death "Direct Funeral" or "Direct Cremation" is quickly requested then less money can be paid but the funeral or burial may be done without family present and watching. Everyone basically should do the funeral, burial, and related things a person wanted if a decedent's estate can afford it.

SIGN FORM WITH NOTARY AND 2 WITNESSES

The form to be completed must be signed by the person doing the form and 2 witnesses while they are in front of a person who is a notary who then notarizes the form. Witnesses must be at least 18 and can't be named in the form or, also, work in funeral or related fields. People should keep the form in a place so it will be found <u>quickly within 1 or 2 days of a person's death</u>. A person can cancel the form by ripping it up, throwing it away, or clearly saying so, and then maybe telling all persons who have been shown the form.

COMMONWEALTH OF KENTUCKY
OFFICE OF THE ATTORNEY GENERAL

FUNERAL PLANNING DECLARATION
FORM FPD-1, 04-17

Declaration made this _____ day of _____ (month, year). I, _____ (print name, also referred to as "Declarant" in this Declaration), being at least eighteen (18) years of age and of sound mind, willfully and voluntarily make known my instructions concerning funeral services, funeral and cemetery merchandise, ceremonies, and the disposition of my remains after my death. By executing this Declaration, I revoke any Declaration previously made.

Designee
1. A Designee is an individual designated and directed by the terms of this Declaration to carry out the Declarant's funeral plan or make arrangements concerning disposition of the Declarant's remains, funeral services, cemetery merchandise, funeral merchandise, or ceremonies;
2. If the Declarant does not designate a Designee in this Declaration, the Declarant shall provide instructions concerning funeral services, ceremonies, and disposition of the Declarant's remains;
3. A person is not considered to be entitled to any part of the Declarant's estate solely by virtue of being designated in this Declaration to serve as the Designee;
4. The Designee shall not be a provider of funeral or cemetery services, or employed by any entity responsible for providing funeral or cemetery services or disposing of the Declarant's remains, unless the Designee is related to the Declarant by birth, marriage or adoption;
5. A Designee shall not be a witness to this Declaration;
6. If the Designee or alternate Designee fail to assume an obligation set forth in this Declaration, within five (5) days of notification of the Declarant's death, the authority to make arrangements shall devolve pursuant to the terms of this Declaration or KRS 367.93117.

_____ I hereby declare and direct that after my death _____ (name of Designee) shall, as my Designee, carry out the instructions that are set forth in this Declaration. If my Designee is unwilling or unable to act, I declare _____ (name of alternate Designee) as an alternate Designee.

_____ I hereby elect not to select a Designee, and direct that the instructions listed herein for funeral services, ceremonies, and the disposition of my remains after my death be followed.

Instructions Concerning Funeral Services, Funeral and Cemetery Merchandise, Ceremonies, and the Disposition of My Remains After My Death

I hereby declare and direct that after my death the following actions be taken (indicate your choice by initialing or making your mark before signing this declaration:

(1) My body shall be (select one):

    (A) ____ Buried. I direct that my body be buried at _____.

    (B) ____ Cremated. I direct that my cremated remains be disposed of as follows, or if no method of disposition is selected then I leave the decision to my Designee:
        ____ Placing them in a grave, crypt, or niche at _____, or if left blank then at a location to be selected by my Designee;
        ____ Scattering them in a scattering area; or
        ____ On private property with the consent of the owner.

    (C) ____ Entombed. I direct that my body be entombed at _____.

    (D) ____ Donated. I direct that my body be donated as an anatomical gift pursuant to KRS 311.1911, et. seq. (Do not select if donation has been selected by another method).

    (E) ____ I intentionally make no decision concerning the disposition of my body, leaving the decision to my Designee.

(2) My arrangements shall be made as follows:

    (A) ____ I direct that funeral services be obtained from (if left blank then my Designee will decide): _____

    (B) ____ I direct that the following funeral services and ceremonial arrangements be made:
    _____
    _____

    (C) ____ I direct the selection of a grave memorial, monument or marker, as follows:
    _____

    (D) ____ I direct that the following funeral and cemetery merchandise and other property be selected for the disposition of my remains, my funeral or other ceremonial arrangements:
    _____
    _____

    (E) ____ I direct my Designee make all arrangements concerning ceremonies and other funeral or burial services.

(3) ____ In addition to the instructions listed above, I request the following:

_____

_____

(4) I direct my Designee to make alternate arrangements to the best of the Designee's ability if it is impossible to make an arrangement specified herein because:
   (A) A funeral home or other service or merchandise provider is out of business, impossible to locate, or otherwise unable to provide the specified service; or
   (B) The specified arrangement is impossible, illegal, or exceeds the funds available or is inconsistent with the terms of the pre-arranged funeral or cemetery contract.

    It is my intention that this Declaration be honored by my family and others as the final expression of my intentions concerning my funeral and the disposition of my body after my death. I understand the full import of this Declaration.

Signatures   **The following signatures and notary signature all need to be obtained:**

Declarant, or another person in the Declarant's presence and at the Declarant's direction

Signed: _____ Date: _____

Declarant's City, County, and State of Residence: _____

Print name of person who signed at Declarant's direction (if applicable): _____

Witnesses
    I believe the Declarant to be of sound mind and willfully and voluntarily executed the Declaration. I did not sign the Declaration on behalf of and at the direction of the Declarant. I am not a Designee of the Declarant. The Declarant, or the person signing at the direction of the Declarant, signed the Declaration in my presence. I am competent and at least eighteen (18) years of age.

Witness _____   Witness _____
Printed Name _____   Printed Name _____
Date _____   Date _____

Notary Public or other person authorized to administer oaths
    State of Kentucky
    _____County
    Before me, the undersigned authority, came the Declarant and acknowledged that he or she voluntarily dated and signed this writing, or directed it to be signed and dated as above in his or her presence, on this the _____ day of _____, 20____.

_____   My Commission Expires: _____
Notary Public or other person authorized
to administer oaths   Title: _____

APPENDIX: SAMPLE FILLED OUT FORMS

TO GET FORMS TO USE PEOPLE CAN:
   (1) PHOTOCOPY BOOK PAGES,
   (2) TEAR OUT PAGES FROM A BOOK, OR
   (3) DOWNLOAD BOOK WITH FORMS FROM WWW.DAVENPORTPUBLISHING.COM
AND USUALLY PDF FORM AT IS BEST TO AVOID SPACING/FORMAT CHANGES.

EMAIL ANY COMMENTS TO DAVENPORTPRESS@GMAIL.COM.

On the next pages to show how it can be done are some sample filled out legal forms.

People can add words to legal forms by computer or typewriter to be neater, but many people just by hand use pen, marker, or pencil to handwrite words into forms.

It is not required but is bit better if signatures are in ink or marker not pencil.

Many parts of the forms especially Will gifts can be left empty and unfilled.

Anyone can fill in words in legal form not just the person doing the form, like a friend with neat writing can fill in all the words, addresses, and dates that are needed. Only the final signatures must be done by each person who wants the form.

To add words in form by pen, pencil, typewriter, or computer any of these is fine:
        "I appoint ___*John Doe*___ as Agent",
        "I appoint ___John Doe___ as Agent",
        "I appoint John Doe as Agent".

When doing forms it may help to know "respectively" means "in order just stated".

People need not worry about neatness or small mistakes, and a document is usually fine if those people who knew a decedent in life can tell the likely meaning.

==Sample Filled Out Form: Will (Standard)==
==with Gifts section skipped to not bother making small gifts==

LAST WILL AND TESTAMENT

I, _Paul Samuel Maxwell_, of _Forsyth County_, Kentucky, do revoke all prior Wills and testamentary documents and do make, publish, and declare this as my Will. I am of sound mind and under no duress or undue influence and act voluntarily.

1. LIVING SPOUSE AND CHILDREN. To show I am mentally fit and have sufficient memory to do a Will I do say I now have the following living spouse and living children:

_____ none _____
_____.

2. GIFTS. I give these gifts in this Will, but to get a gift in this section the recipient must survive me except as otherwise stated below.

I give _____ to _____.
I give _____ to _____.
I give _____ to _____.
I give _____ to _____.
I give _____ to _____.
I give _____ to _____.
I give _____ to _____.
I give _____ to _____.
I give _____ to _____.
I give _____ to _____.
I give _____ to _____.

SKIPPED

3. RESIDUE. The rest, residue, and remainder of my estate, and anything else, I give:

  a) to _Susan Maxwell_____ who survive me and with persons just named who survive me taking the share of non-survivors, then if anything remains

  b) to _Oscar Adam Maxwell and Mary Ann Tabor_ and if any of those just now named do not survive me their part goes to their lineal descendants per stirpes.

55

4. ADMINISTRATION. I name, nominate, and appoint _Susan Maxwell my sister_ as Personal Representative including for me, my Will, and my estate.

5. MISCELLANEOUS. The following applies to this Will and generally.

In this Will no part left unfilled is a mistake including spaces in the residue clause.

The facts support and I want Kentucky law to apply to this Will and my estate.

I order that my just debts, funeral and related expenses, and taxes be paid as soon after my death as practical but only those items my Personal Representative chooses to pay.

Priority of Will gifts of the same type is based on the order they are made in this Will.

The words give and gift also means a devise, bequest, grant, legacy, or similar.

I am intentionally not providing by Will or other ways for some family, including I am not providing for some children of mine and also children of a deceased child of mine.

If a Will gift reasonably mentions survival then survival is an absolute condition and anti-lapse laws or similar provisions have no effect and without survival the gift lapses. Unless a Will gift specifies otherwise if a Will gift goes to multiple recipients if any do not survive me the part to them lapses and instead goes to other surviving recipients.

No earlier transfer reduces a Will gift unless I usually called it a loan or advancement.

In this Will any gendered word includes all genders, and the singular includes the plural and vice versa, and they can mean a single person or many persons.

Unless a Will specifically says otherwise a secured debt including a mortgage or lien shall not be paid off including by a Personal Representative or in probate, and a recipient of a Will gift of property takes it subject to debts. Also, no recipient of property who may lose it or who pays to keep it may have my estate or others pay or do exoneration.

If I somehow lost ownership of an item in a specific Will gift the gift is extinguished.

I request and authorize any informal, summary, and quick probate or similar action. Any Personal Representative may act independently with no supervision of any court, including independent administration, and with no inventory, appraisal, or other action.

I give any Personal Representative the a) fullest authority, discretion, and powers allowed by state law, b) power to lease, sell, mortgage, convey, or keep property including real property in a manner and time they deem helpful or proper, and c) authority to settle or pay claims or debts in the time and manner they choose. Any Personal Representative or other fiduciary shall have all powers and authorities that may be given by statute or common law in any jurisdiction they may act, including under Kentucky law.

Any Guardian of any type, Conservator, Custodian, or other person managing a minor's property or money may use or invade the principal and sell property without court action.

If context permits the terms Personal Representative and Executor and Administrator are interchangeable, Conservator and Guardian of the Estate and Guardian of Property and Custodian are interchangeable, and residue and residuary are interchangeable. Any such person may stand in the place of and have all powers like the others named here.

The residue includes lapsed or failed gifts, insurance paid to the estate, digital assets, inheritances owed me, and all I had power of appointment or testamentary disposition over.

Any Personal Representative may access, manage, delete, modify, transfer, and otherwise control any digital accounts and assets I had any interest in or power over.

Any Personal Representative, Executor, Administrator, Guardian of any type like for a person or estate, Conservator, Custodian, and any other fiduciary under this Will or otherwise shall qualify and serve without bond, surety, security, surety bond, or similar.

If evidence does not show it likely a person survived me by 120 hours (5 days) then for this Will and my estate they shall be deemed in all ways as having died before me.

Any Personal Representative may at any time transfer money or property of a minor under age 18 to a Custodian to act under the Kentucky Uniform Transfers to Minors Act or similar law anywhere, and may pick a person to be Custodian including themselves.

If part of this Will is by law invalid or unenforceable other provisions remain in effect.

TESTATOR

IN WITNESS WHEREOF, I, _Paul Samuel Maxwell_, the Testator, on the _8th_ day of _January_, 20_23_, sign my name to this instrument and do hereby declare that I sign and execute this instrument as my Will and that I sign it willingly, that I execute it as my free and voluntary act for the purposes expressed in it, and that I am 18 years of age or older, of sound mind, and under no constraint or undue influence.

Paul Samuel Maxwell
Signature of Testator

WITNESSES

We, _Susan Ann Moon_ and _Eve Mable Smith_, the Witnesses, on the date indicated above, sign our names to this instrument, and do hereby declare that the Testator signs and executes this instrument as the Will of the Testator and that the Testator signs it willingly, that each of us in the presence and hearing of the Testator and the other Witness who is signing hereby signs this Will to act as witnesses to the Testator's signing, and to the best of our knowledge the Testator is 18 years of age or older, of sound mind, and under no constraint or undue influence.

Susan Ann Moon　　　　　　　_14 2nd Street, Louisville, KY 42203_
Signature of Witness #1　　　　Address of Witness #1

Eve Mable Smith　　　　　　　_35 Buffalo Road, Denver, Colorado 80101_
Signature of Witness #2　　　　Address of Witness #2

Sample Filled Out Form: Will (Guardian)
with many gifts written in Gifts section, Guardian Clause used, and Residue Clause using percentages

LAST WILL AND TESTAMENT

I, __Paul Brian Baker__ of __Jefferson County__, Kentucky, do revoke all prior Wills and testamentary documents and do make, publish, and declare this as my Will. I am of sound mind and under no duress or undue influence and act voluntarily.

1. LIVING SPOUSE AND CHILDREN. To show I am mentally fit and have sufficient memory to do a Will I do say I now have the following living spouse and living children:
_____ Ruth May Baker wife _____ Oscar Elliot Baker young son _____
_____ Karen Lisa Lundy daughter _____ Derek Rupert Baker son _____.

2. GIFTS. I give these gifts in this Will, but to get a gift in this section the recipient must survive me except as otherwise stated below.

I give __big oak table__ to __Anne J. Smith__.

I give __$5,000 and Ford Truck__ to __Loretta Marsha Baxter__.

I give __buildings, land, and fixtures at 63 Wentworth Road, Lexington, Kentucky,__ to __Kenneth Alan Ford__.

I give __all real property and fixtures I own in Fayette County in Kentucky__ to __Amy Marie Fox and Pamela Sue Fox__.

I give __903 Iceberg Road, Anchorage, Alaska__ to __James Eric Hanson__.

I give __Irish jewelry and my wedding ring__ to __Mary Natalie Swanson__.

I give __all jewelry not given above__ to __Kay Baxter__ and __Mary Baxter__.

I give __$781.35__ to __Mary Natalie Swanson and Kevin Kilby__.

I give __Wells Fargo acct ending in #8923__ to __Lawrence Deer a hunting buddy__.

I give __all spare tires and auto parts__ to __Victor Perez my mechanic__.

3. RESIDUE. The rest, residue, and remainder of my estate, and anything else, I give:
a) to __Ruth May Baker__ who survive me and with persons just named who survive me taking the share of non-survivors, then if anything remains
b) to __50% to Oscar Elliot Baker, 35% to Karen Lisa Lundy, 5% to Mary Sue Baker, and 10% to Luis Sanchez my friend__ and if any of those just now named do not survive me their part goes to their lineal descendants per stirpes.

4. ADMINISTRATION. I name, nominate, and appoint ___Ruth May Baker___
as Personal Representative including for me, my Will, and my estate.

5. GUARDIAN. I name ___Amanda Sue Brubaker my sister___ to be Guardian of
any minor child of mine and to have care, authority, custody, and other control of them.
The person just named above shall also act as Guardian in all matters involving any minor
child's property, money, and estate and they shall have care, control, and power over these
things (including as Conservator if this is helpful).

6. MISCELLANEOUS. The following applies to this Will and generally.

In this Will no part left unfilled is a mistake including spaces in the residue clause.

The facts support and I want Kentucky law to apply to this Will and my estate.

I order that my just debts, funeral and related expenses, and taxes be paid as soon after
my death as practical but only those items my Personal Representative chooses to pay.

Priority of Will gifts of the same type is based on the order they are made in this Will.

The words give and gift also means a devise, bequest, grant, legacy, or similar.

I am intentionally not providing by Will or other ways for some family, including I am
not providing for some children of mine and also children of a deceased child of mine.

If a Will gift reasonably mentions survival then survival is an absolute condition and
anti-lapse laws or similar provisions have no effect and without survival the gift lapses.
Unless a Will gift specifies otherwise if a Will gift goes to multiple recipients if any
do not survive me the part to them lapses and instead goes to other surviving recipients.

No earlier transfer reduces a Will gift unless I usually called it a loan or advancement.

In this Will any gendered word includes all genders, and the singular includes the
plural and vice versa, and they can mean a single person or many persons.

Unless a Will specifically says otherwise a secured debt including a mortgage or lien
shall not be paid off including by a Personal Representative or in probate, and a recipient
of a Will gift of property takes it subject to debts. Also, no recipient of property who may
lose it or who pays to keep it may have my estate or others pay or do exoneration.

If I somehow lost ownership of an item in a specific Will gift the gift is extinguished.

I request and authorize any informal, summary, and quick probate or similar action.
Any Personal Representative may act independently with no supervision of any court,
including independent administration, and with no inventory, appraisal, or other action.

I give any Personal Representative the a) fullest authority, discretion, and powers
allowed by state law, b) power to lease, sell, mortgage, convey, or keep property including
real property in a manner and time they deem helpful or proper, and c) authority to settle or
pay claims or debts in the time and manner they choose. Any Personal Representative or
other fiduciary shall have all powers and authorities that may be given by statute or
common law in any jurisdiction they may act, including under Kentucky law.

Any Guardian of any type, Conservator, Custodian, or other person managing a minor's
property or money may use or invade the principal and sell property without court action.

If context permits the terms Personal Representative and Executor and Administrator

are interchangeable, Conservator and Guardian of the Estate and Guardian of Property and Custodian are interchangeable, and residue and residuary are interchangeable. Any such person may stand in the place of and have all powers like the others named here.

The residue includes lapsed or failed gifts, insurance paid to the estate, digital assets, inheritances owed me, and all I had power of appointment or testamentary disposition over.

Any Personal Representative may access, manage, delete, modify, transfer, and otherwise control any digital accounts and assets I had any interest in or power over.

Any Personal Representative, Executor, Administrator, Guardian of any type like for a person or estate, Conservator, Custodian, and any other fiduciary under this Will or otherwise shall qualify and serve without bond, surety, security, surety bond, or similar.

If evidence does not show it likely a person survived me by 120 hours (5 days) then for this Will and my estate they shall be deemed in all ways as having died before me.

Any Personal Representative may at any time transfer money or property of a minor under age 18 to a Custodian to act under the Kentucky Uniform Transfers to Minors Act or similar law anywhere, and may pick a person to be Custodian including themselves.

If part of this Will is by law invalid or unenforceable other provisions remain in effect.

TESTATOR

IN WITNESS WHEREOF, I, __*Paul Brian Baker*__ , the Testator, on the __15th__ day of __*March*__, 20 __19__, sign my name to this instrument and do hereby declare that I sign and execute this instrument as my Will and that I sign it willingly, that I execute it as my free and voluntary act for the purposes expressed in it, and that I am 18 years of age or older, of sound mind, and under no constraint or undue influence.

Paul Brian Baker
Signature of Testator

WITNESSES

We, __*Olivia Anna Paulson*__ and __*Matthew John Paulson*__, the Witnesses, on the date indicated above, sign our names to this instrument, and do hereby declare that the Testator signs and executes this instrument as the Will of the Testator and that the Testator signs it willingly, that each of us in the presence and hearing of the Testator and the other Witness who is signing hereby signs this Will to act as witnesses to the Testator's signing, and to the best of our knowledge the Testator is 18 years of age or older, of sound mind, and under no constraint or undue influence.

Olivia Anna Paulson   __82 Forest Road, Glasgow, KY 41204__
Signature of Witness #1   Address of Witness #1

Matthew John Paulson   __82 Forest Road, Glasgow, KY 41204__
Signature of Witness #2   Address of Witness #2

**Sample Filled Out Form : Will (Guardian)
with Gifts section left unused and, then,
the Residue Clause done only using 2nd space so as to
gift to all branches of person's descendants equally**

LAST WILL AND TESTAMENT

I, ___Thomas Roger Tedford___ of ___Boone County___ , Kentucky, do revoke all prior Wills and testamentary documents and do make, publish, and declare this as my Will. I am of sound mind and under no duress or undue influence and act voluntarily.

1. LIVING SPOUSE AND CHILDREN. To show I am mentally fit and have sufficient memory to do a Will I do say I now have the following living spouse and living children:

__Mary Paula Tedford my daughter_____Gina Lola Smith my daughter_____

_____.

2. GIFTS. I give these gifts in this Will, but to get a gift in this section the recipient must survive me except as otherwise stated below.

I give _____ to _____.

I give _____ to _____.

I give _____ to _____.

I give _____ to _____.

I give _____ to _____.

I give _____ to _____.

I give _____ to _____.

I give _____ to _____.

3. RESIDUE. The rest, residue, and remainder of my estate, and anything else, I give:

   a) to _____ who survive me and with persons just named who survive me taking the share of non-survivors, then if anything remains

   b) to _Brian Alan Tedford my deceased son,_ _Mary Paula Tedford my daughter,_ and _____Gina Lola Smith my daughter_____ and if any of those just now named do not survive me their part goes to their lineal descendants per stirpes.

4. ADMINISTRATION. I name, nominate, and appoint __Mary Paula Tedford__ as Personal Representative including for me, my Will, and my estate.

5. MISCELLANEOUS. The following applies to this Will and generally.

In this Will no part left unfilled is a mistake including spaces in the residue clause.

The facts support and I want Kentucky law to apply to this Will and my estate.

I order that my just debts, funeral and related expenses, and taxes be paid as soon after my death as practical but only those items my Personal Representative chooses to pay.

Priority of Will gifts of the same type is based on the order they are made in this Will.

The words give and gift also means a devise, bequest, grant, legacy, or similar.

I am intentionally not providing by Will or other ways for some family, including I am not providing for some children of mine and also children of a deceased child of mine.

If a Will gift reasonably mentions survival then survival is an absolute condition and anti-lapse laws or similar provisions have no effect and without survival the gift lapses. Unless a Will gift specifies otherwise if a Will gift goes to multiple recipients if any do not survive me the part to them lapses and instead goes to other surviving recipients.

No earlier transfer reduces a Will gift unless I usually called it a loan or advancement.

In this Will any gendered word includes all genders, and the singular includes the plural and vice versa, and they can mean a single person or many persons.

Unless a Will specifically says otherwise a secured debt including a mortgage or lien shall not be paid off including by a Personal Representative or in probate, and a recipient of a Will gift of property takes it subject to debts. Also, no recipient of property who may lose it or who pays to keep it may have my estate or others pay or do exoneration.

If I somehow lost ownership of an item in a specific Will gift the gift is extinguished.

I request and authorize any informal, summary, and quick probate or similar action. Any Personal Representative may act independently with no supervision of any court, including independent administration, and with no inventory, appraisal, or other action.

I give any Personal Representative the a) fullest authority, discretion, and powers allowed by state law, b) power to lease, sell, mortgage, convey, or keep property including real property in a manner and time they deem helpful or proper, and c) authority to settle or pay claims or debts in the time and manner they choose. Any Personal Representative or other fiduciary shall have all powers and authorities that may be given by statute or common law in any jurisdiction they may act, including under Kentucky law.

Any Guardian of any type, Conservator, Custodian, or other person managing a minor's property or money may use or invade the principal and sell property without court action.

If context permits the terms Personal Representative and Executor and Administrator are interchangeable, Conservator and Guardian of the Estate and Guardian of Property and Custodian are interchangeable, and residue and residuary are interchangeable. Any such person may stand in the place of and have all powers like the others named here.

The residue includes lapsed or failed gifts, insurance paid to the estate, digital assets,

inheritances owed me, and all I had power of appointment or testamentary disposition over.

Any Personal Representative may access, manage, delete, modify, transfer, and otherwise control any digital accounts and assets I had any interest in or power over.

Any Personal Representative, Executor, Administrator, Guardian of any type like for a person or estate, Conservator, Custodian, and any other fiduciary under this Will or otherwise shall qualify and serve without bond, surety, security, surety bond, or similar.

If evidence does not show it likely a person survived me by 120 hours (5 days) then for this Will and my estate they shall be deemed in all ways as having died before me.

Any Personal Representative may at any time transfer money or property of a minor under age 18 to a Custodian to act under the Kentucky Uniform Transfers to Minors Act or similar law anywhere, and may pick a person to be Custodian including themselves.

If part of this Will is by law invalid or unenforceable other provisions remain in effect.

TESTATOR

IN WITNESS WHEREOF, I, _Thomas Roger Tedford_, the Testator, on the _22nd_ day of _July_, 20_23_, sign my name to this instrument and do hereby declare that I sign and execute this instrument as my Will and that I sign it willingly, that I execute it as my free and voluntary act for the purposes expressed in it, and that I am 18 years of age or older, of sound mind, and under no constraint or undue influence.

Thomas Roger Tedford
Signature of Testator

WITNESSES

We, _Maria Bonita Buena_ and _Richard Max West_, the Witnesses, on the date indicated above, sign our names to this instrument, and do hereby declare that the Testator signs and executes this instrument as the Will of the Testator and that the Testator signs it willingly, that each of us in the presence and hearing of the Testator and the other Witness who is signing hereby signs this Will to act as witnesses to the Testator's signing, and to the best of our knowledge the Testator is 18 years of age or older, of sound mind, and under no constraint or undue influence.

Maria Bonita Buena   _101 Fox Rd., Apt. #35 Clayton, KY 41003_
Signature of Witness #1   Address of Witness #1

Richard Max West   _28 Miller Avenue, Pineville, KY 41142_
Signature of Witness #2   Address of Witness #2

Sample Filled Out Form : Will (Standard) with Will modified to have a 1 Part Residue Clause

LAST WILL AND TESTAMENT

I, __John David Smith__, of __Kenton County__, Kentucky, do revoke all prior Wills and testamentary documents and do make, publish, and declare this as my Will. I am of sound mind and under no duress or undue influence and act voluntarily.

1. LIVING SPOUSE AND CHILDREN. To show I am mentally fit and have sufficient memory to do a Will I do say I now have the following living spouse and living children: __my son Adam Michael Smith__.

2. GIFTS. I give these gifts in this Will, but to get a gift in this section the recipient must survive me except as otherwise stated below.

I give __$200__ to __each of my nieces and nephews so about $2,800 in total__.

I give __$400__ to __Garner Food Shelf in Bowling Green, Kentucky by city hall__.

I give __$340__ to __my old church Trinity Catholic Church in Pueblo, Colorado__.

I give _____ to _____.

I give _____ to _____.

I give _____ to _____.

I give _____ to _____.

I give _____ to _____.

I give _____ to _____.

I give _____ to _____.

I give _____ to _____.

3. RESIDUE. The rest, residue, and remainder of my estate, and anything else, I give to: __Adam Michael Smith__ and __Judy Paula Ford__ who survive me and if any of those just named do not survive me their part goes to their lineal descendants per stirpes.

4. ADMINISTRATION. I name, nominate, and appoint <u>Judy Paula Ford my sister</u>
as Personal Representative including for me, my Will, and my estate.

5. MISCELLANEOUS. The following applies to this Will and generally.

In this Will no part left unfilled is a mistake including spaces in the residue clause.

The facts support and I want Kentucky law to apply to this Will and my estate.

I order that my just debts, funeral and related expenses, and taxes be paid as soon after my death as practical but only those items my Personal Representative chooses to pay.

Priority of Will gifts of the same type is based on the order they are made in this Will.

The words give and gift also means a devise, bequest, grant, legacy, or similar.

I am intentionally not providing by Will or other ways for some family, including I am not providing for some children of mine and also children of a deceased child of mine.

If a Will gift reasonably mentions survival then survival is an absolute condition and anti-lapse laws or similar provisions have no effect and without survival the gift lapses. Unless a Will gift specifies otherwise if a Will gift goes to multiple recipients if any do not survive me the part to them lapses and instead goes to other surviving recipients.

No earlier transfer reduces a Will gift unless I usually called it a loan or advancement.

In this Will any gendered word includes all genders, and the singular includes the plural and vice versa, and they can mean a single person or many persons.

Unless a Will specifically says otherwise a secured debt including a mortgage or lien shall not be paid off including by a Personal Representative or in probate, and a recipient of a Will gift of property takes it subject to debts. Also, no recipient of property who may lose it or who pays to keep it may have my estate or others pay or do exoneration.

If I somehow lost ownership of an item in a specific Will gift the gift is extinguished.

I request and authorize any informal, summary, and quick probate or similar action. Any Personal Representative may act independently with no supervision of any court, including independent administration, and with no inventory, appraisal, or other action.

I give any Personal Representative the a) fullest authority, discretion, and powers allowed by state law, b) power to lease, sell, mortgage, convey, or keep property including real property in a manner and time they deem helpful or proper, and c) authority to settle or pay claims or debts in the time and manner they choose. Any Personal Representative or other fiduciary shall have all powers and authorities that may be given by statute or common law in any jurisdiction they may act, including under Kentucky law.

Any Guardian of any type, Conservator, Custodian, or other person managing a minor's property or money may use or invade the principal and sell property without court action.

If context permits the terms Personal Representative and Executor and Administrator are interchangeable, Conservator and Guardian of the Estate and Guardian of Property and Custodian are interchangeable, and residue and residuary are interchangeable. Any such person may stand in the place of and have all powers like the others named here.

The residue includes lapsed or failed gifts, insurance paid to the estate, digital assets, inheritances owed me, and all I had power of appointment or testamentary disposition over.

Any Personal Representative may access, manage, delete, modify, transfer, and otherwise control any digital accounts and assets I had any interest in or power over.

Any Personal Representative, Executor, Administrator, Guardian of any type like for a person or estate, Conservator, Custodian, and any other fiduciary under this Will or otherwise shall qualify and serve without bond, surety, security, surety bond, or similar.

If evidence does not show it likely a person survived me by 120 hours (5 days) then for this Will and my estate they shall be deemed in all ways as having died before me.

Any Personal Representative may at any time transfer money or property of a minor under age 18 to a Custodian to act under the Kentucky Uniform Transfers to Minors Act or similar law anywhere, and may pick a person to be Custodian including themselves.

If part of this Will is by law invalid or unenforceable other provisions remain in effect.

TESTATOR

IN WITNESS WHEREOF, I, __John David Smith__, the Testator, on the __30th__ day of __December__, 20__19__, sign my name to this instrument and do hereby declare that I sign and execute this instrument as my Will and that I sign it willingly, that I execute it as my free and voluntary act for the purposes expressed in it, and that I am 18 years of age or older, of sound mind, and under no constraint or undue influence.

_____*John David Smith*_____
Signature of Testator

WITNESSES

We, __Mark Elliot Potter__ and __Ann Paula Blom__, the Witnesses, on the date indicated above, sign our names to this instrument, and do hereby declare that the Testator signs and executes this instrument as the Will of the Testator and that the Testator signs it willingly, that each of us in the presence and hearing of the Testator and the other Witness who is signing hereby signs this Will to act as witnesses to the Testator's signing, and to the best of our knowledge the Testator is 18 years of age or older, of sound mind, and under no constraint or undue influence.

Mark Elliot Potter   24 Spruce St, Sherwood, KY 41212
Signature of Witness #1   Address of Witness #1

Ann Paula Blom   80 Oak Ave., Edison, Kentucky 40028
Signature of Witness #2   Address of Witness #2

Sample Filled Out Form : Self-Proving Affidavit

SELF-PROVING AFFIDAVIT

STATE OF KENTUCKY

COUNTY OF __KENTON COUNTY__

    Before me, the undersigned authority, on this day personally appeared __John David Smith__ and __Mark Elliot Potter and Ann Paula Blom__, known to me to be the Testator and the Witnesses, respectively, whose names are signed to the attached or foregoing instrument and, all of these persons being by me first duly sworn. __John David Smith__, the Testator, declared to me and to the Witnesses in my presence that the instrument is the Will of the Testator and the Testator had willingly signed or directed another to sign for the Testator, and that the Testator executed it as Testator's free and voluntary act for the purposes therein expressed; and each of the Witnesses stated to me, in the presence and hearing of the Testator, that each Witness signed the Will to act as witness in the presence of the Testator and of the other subscribing Witness, and that to the best of the knowledge of each Witness the Testator was 18 years of age or over, of sound mind and under no constraint or undue influence.

John David Smith
Testator

Mark Elliot Potter
Witness

Ann Paula Blom
Witness

Subscribed, sworn and acknowledged before me by __John David Smith__, the Testator, subscribed and sworn before me by __Mark Elliot Potter__ and __Ann Paula Blom__ the Witnesses, this __30th__ day of __December__, 20__19__,

Matthew L. Galvez
Signature
Official Capacity Of Officer: _____

> **MATTHEW L. GALVEZ**
> NOTARY PUBLIC
> STATE AT LARGE, KENTUCKY
> COMM. # 31435624983
> MY COMMISSION EXPIRES APRIL 7, 2038